JOHN L. STODDARD'S LECTURES

FLORENCE   NAPLES

ROME

Norwood Press
J. S. Cushing & Co. — Berwick & Smith
Norwood, Mass., U.S.A.

Macdonald & Sons, Bookbinders, Boston

L.BRAONHOLD.

JOHN L. STODDARD'S
LECTURES

ILLUSTRATED AND EMBELLISHED WITH VIEWS OF THE
WORLD'S FAMOUS PLACES AND PEOPLE, BEING
THE IDENTICAL DISCOURSES DELIVERED
DURING THE PAST EIGHTEEN
YEARS UNDER THE TITLE
OF THE STODDARD
LECTURES

COMPLETE IN TEN VOLUMES

VOL. VIII

BOSTON
BALCH BROTHERS CO.
MDCCCXCVIII

FLORENCE

FLORENCE

" I LIKE a well-made, modern building better than any ruin in the world." "And I would rather see a ruin, if it possessed historic interest, than the best modern structure ever framed." They were Americans, walking the deck of an Atlantic steamer. Both were intelligent, outspoken, and sincere. They represented in these words two widely different classes of their fellow-countrymen. The first speaker expressed the view of those who are intensely practical and progressive. They are " weary of kings," emancipated from the past, impatient of Old-World conservatism, and so exultant in the building up of new and prosperous communities that they consider it almost sacrilege to waste their time on men, events, and buildings of antiquity. The second represented those Americans whose patriotism is no less strong than that of the first-mentioned class, and who concede that the Old World looks rather toward the Past, while the New World is

LEONARDO DA VINCI.

gazing toward the Future. They cannot forget, however, that we are the descendants of the Ages, and that, as Lowell admirably says, " Ride fast and far as we may, we carry the Past on our crupper, as immovably seated there as the black Care of the Roman poet." That Americans should desire to travel

SAVONAROLA.

abroad is not, therefore, as some are wont to say, indicative either of a want of patriotism or of a foolish effort to be fashionable.

A justifiable and even praiseworthy motive for a foreign tour is the wish to see with our own eyes, and to tread with our own feet, places which make the great events of History, the heroes of Biography, and the masterpieces of Art more vivid to our consciousness than they can ever be while a great ocean intervenes, and they are merely read of and imagined. Hence, all who visit the Old World with true, appreciative interest, are really pilgrims to the homes of genius, shrines of art, sites of epoch-making action, and tombs of the illustrious dead. Moreover, this desire, though naturally strongest among us of the New World, is shared by lovers of the

FLORENCE FROM THE SQUARE OF MICHELANGELO.

historic and the beautiful in every land. Whatever be their language, nationality, or faith, all students of the Past are heirs together in the heritage of History; and under the broad dome of heaven the homes of noble minds and the scenes of heroic deeds become our universal sanctuaries.

One of the most important of these sanctuaries is Florence, the cradle of the Renaissance. Reclining in her amphitheatre of vine-clad hills, cleft by the golden current of the Arno, and guarded by the Tuscan Apennines, Florence is not alone one of the most attractive cities in the world, she is a beacon light of history. How priceless is the debt of gratitude we owe her! After the appalling gloom of the Dark Ages which, on

THE PERSEUS OF CELLINI.

the downfall of Imperial Rome, enfolded Europe like a shroud, the first pale streaks of light, announcing the dawn of a new age, appeared above the towers of this Tuscan Athens. It is true, the glory which succeeded that bright dawn did not last long; but during its continuance Italian art and literature reached their zenith, and Florence ever since has been a treasure-house for those who prize inspiring memories and forms which, though imprisoned upon canvas or in marble, seem endowed with life.

The place toward which the visitor to Florence usually first directs his steps is the Square of the Senate, where, with mingled feelings of awe and pleasure, he recognizes the imposing form of the Palazzo Vecchio, or Old Palace, which has been standing here in massive grandeur for six hundred years. It served as the Senate-House during the Republic, and afterward as the official residence of the Medici, — that famous family which gave eight dukes to Tuscany, two queens to France, and four popes to the Vatican. The shadow of its stately tower fell upon this Florentine forum two hundred years before Columbus sailed for the New World; and, every day since then, has traced its sombre path-

THE PALAZZO VECCHIO.

way on the ancient pavement, as if Fate's "moving finger" were writing there the city's destiny in lines which none can understand. What an amount of history these frowning battlements enclose! Thus, in the lofty tower there may still be seen a dismal cell possessing mournful interest, as having been for forty days the prison of Savonarola, whose delicate frame was racked with anguish from the torture to which he was at intervals subjected.

Only a few years since, there was discovered in this tower an opening into a secret shaft, communicating with a black pit two hundred feet below; and no doubt many a prisoner, as he came down the staircase from the tower dungeon, was suddenly pushed through the aperture into it, to fall with a wild shriek

THE COURTYARD OF THE PALAZZO VECCHIO.

of horror, through the darkness, to an unknown, subterranean tomb. Poor Savonarola was, at least, spared such an ignominious and mysterious exit from the world; for these old palace walls, in 1498, were reddened by the glare of the reformer's burning form, and echoed to the curses of the fickle multitude which had so often listened spellbound to his words when he virtually ruled the Florentine Republic from his pulpit, but which, that day, as eagerly thronged every window, roof, and balcony in the vicinity to witness his death agony. Yet, when the reaction came, this same Palazzo Vecchio, above the gate of which Savonarola had affixed the words, "Jesus Christ is the King

SAVONAROLA.

of Florence," beheld for centuries, annually, on the anniversary of his death, this area strewn with violets, in memory of the good which Savonarola had achieved and in atonement for his martyrdom.

> " For Humanity sweeps onward ; where to-day the martyr stands,
> On the morrow crouches Judas with the silver in his hands.
> Far in front the Cross stands ready and the crackling fagots burn,
> While the hooting mob of yesterday, in silent awe return
> To glean up the scattered ashes into History's golden urn."

From 1504 till 1882, Michelangelo's famous statue of David stood beside the entrance to the Palazzo Vecchio — the situation chosen for it by the sculptor himself — but, after three hundred and seventy-eight years of exposure to the elements, it was thought wiser to remove it to the Academy of Fine Arts. Old travelers, therefore, who revisit Florence miss it sadly as they look for it in its accustomed place; for the David is a statue that one never

THE DAVID.

forgets. Like most of Michelangelo's productions it is a figure of heroic size, and was intended, doubtless, to be placed at a considerable height and to be observed from a distance. As we view the grand proportions and the stern, resolute expression of the youthful shepherd going forth to battle with Goliath, we cannot wonder that the creation of this statue was such an event in Florence that, for many years, it was the custom of the Florentines to reckon

FLORENCE FROM THE HILL.

occurrences as happening so long " after the completion of the David." The work was the more remarkable because its author was obliged to cut it from a block of marble, eighteen feet in length, which had been injured by a clumsy sculptor and had lain useless more than fifty years; but he, struck with its beauty, and longing to achieve what others had believed to be impossible, resolved to carve from the block a colossal statue, representing the future king and psalmist of Israel in the first great crisis of his life. Up to that time, people had been skeptical of Michelangelo's genius; but when, in 1504, this figure had been completed, there was no longer any doubt. He had become the foremost living sculptor of the world.

MICHELANGELO.

One of many anecdotes connected with the David shows that human nature is much the same in all ages. After it had

been placed upon its pedestal, a pompous Florentine official
came to see it and, after deigning to express great admiration
for the work, suggested that the nose appeared to him too large.
Hearing this, Michelangelo gravely mounted a ladder and
pretended to work at the face for a few moments, dropping
meantime some marble dust which he had in his pocket. At
last (having really made no change) he turned with a question-
ing glance to his critic, who responded: " Bravo; bravo; you
have given it life!"

On another side of the Square of the Senate, at right angles
to the Palazzo Vecchio, stands a marble portico of grand proportions. It is called the Loggia of the Lancers, from the
fact that the ducal guard was formerly stationed here; but
the original purpose of its construction was to afford a place of
shelter, where citizens could assemble for the discussion of public affairs. For more than five hundred years, this beautiful
arcade of lofty arches has charmed all visitors to Florence, from
the most casual observer to the accomplished architect. When
Lorenzo de' Medici asked Michelangelo to design another splendid ornament for the square, the sculptor answered: " Carry

THE LOGGIA.

the Loggia entirely around it. Nothing finer can possibly be invented." The duke, however, shrank from the expense of the undertaking. To-day this portico has a nobler use than that of sheltering Medicean lancers, since at present it forms an imposing canopy for works of art, which are so numerous in Florence as to overflow, apparently, from her great sculpture galleries into the streets, where they command the admiration of every passer-by.

THE PORTICO OF THE LANCERS.

Among them are John of Bologna's celebrated work, — the

THE "RAPE OF THE SABINES."

"Rape of the Sabines," and the famous group in bronze by Benvenuto Cellini, representing the hero, Perseus, holding up in triumph the head of the monster, Medusa, whose lifeless body he tramples under foot.

Nor is modern art wanting here. In the rear of Cellini's master-piece stands a magnificent group completed by the Florentine sculptor, Fedi, in 1865. It represents a painful subject in mythology, — the seizure of Polyxena by Achilles. The conqueror, whose form is a superb combination of strength and beauty, is bearing away the captured girl; while at his feet the maiden's brother, who has tried in vain to rescue her, lies in the agony of death. Clinging alike to the relentless captor and her child with feeble hands, is the half-prostrate mother, Hecuba, whose face and attitude are wonderfully effective. The ardor of Achilles is easily comprehended, for the girl's form is of remarkable beauty, none of its rounded outlines being lost beneath the drapery, creased by her struggles into a thousand folds.

POLYXENA AND ACHILLES.

My instinctive admiration of this work was increased when I perceived that, large and complicated as it is, its four figures were carved from a single block of marble. Before producing it, Fedi had toiled for years in poverty and obscurity; but after this achievement, he sprang at a single bound into celebrity, and his masterpiece was placed in the Loggia, as on a throne of honor, among the statues of some of the greatest sculptors of the Renaissance. Moreover, so jealous was Florence of her

new posses-
sion, that she
exacted from
Fedi a promise
never to du-
plicate the
group.

The pro-
duction of a
modern work,
like this of
Fedi, is an ex-
ample of the
indestructible
talent and
fondness for

INSIDE THE LOGGIA.

sculpture which the Italians possess. One day, while lingering
in the Loggia, I saw a little ragged urchin selling flowers. He

MICHELANGELO'S "MOSES."

had the beauti-
ful, pathetic eyes
which are so
rarely seen out-
side of Italy, and
I called him to
me that I might
look admiringly
at them while I
questioned him.

"What do
you wish to be,
when you grow
up to be a man?"
I finally asked.

Without a

moment's hesitation, the little fellow fixed his expressive, lustrous eyes upon me and replied, " *Uno scultore, signore.*"

Close by the Loggia is a narrow passageway, extending from the Palazzo Vecchio to the river Arno, between the parallel arms of the Uffizi Palace, which Medicean princes built to contain the government offices and the archives of the state, together with their vast collection of rare works of art. I felt, however, in no haste to mount the marble staircase of the

PORTICO OF THE UFFIZI.

palace and view its halls of painting and of sculpture. It was enough for me to saunter back and forth in its historic portico, and give my mind completely to the inspiring memories awakened by the place. Such memories readily suggest themselves to any one; for on both sides of this long corridor stand many life-sized marble statues of illustrious Florentines. The figure before which I first halted was that of Leonardo da Vinci. The sight of it fairly thrilled me; for it is one thing to see a portrait of this mighty genius in our homes, and quite another to come suddenly face to face with him, as if in life, within the city of his birth and triumphs. As I surveyed the form of the immortal Leonardo, whose influence in the domain of art was so incalculably great, I felt that it would have been sufficient glory for Florence to have produced this man alone; yet, glancing down the long array of statues, I saw that his was only the commencement of her sculptured heroes. To walk

LEONARDO DA VINCI.

attentively before these marble effigies is to receive a memorable lesson in Italian art and literature; for each of these superbly modeled forms invests with life and personality some name, which may have lain for years half dormant in our memories.

BOCCACCIO.

What a perpetual source of pride and inspiration to the Florentines must these long lines of Masters be, confronting one another thus beneath the portals of this shrine of Art, and looking calmly down upon the crowds that pass and repass constantly between them, with many an upward glance of love and pride! It

AMERIGO VESPUCCI.

stirs the blood of even a stranger from beyond the sea to look upon them; and I should think the sight would make a true-born Florentine as proud of the fair city of his birth, as were the dwellers by the Tiber in the days " when to be a Roman was greater than to be a king"; for in the list of those whom Florence can claim as her own, an entire nation — much more, a single city — might exult.

Among them are Dante, the virtual founder of the Italian language, and one of the three great epic poets of the world; Boccaccio, singer of love; Petrarch, composer of the unrivaled sonnets; Machiavelli, the Mephistopheles of statesmen; Galileo, the astronomer; Brunelleschi, the architect; Giotto, the morning-star of the Renaissance; Guicciardini, the historian; Savonarola, the reformer; Amerigo Vespucci, the discoverer, who gave to our continent his name; Fra Bartolommeo, Andrea del Sarto, and Carlo Dolci, the painters; Benvenuto Cellini, Donatello, and Ghiberti, the sculptors; and last, and greatest of them all, Leonardo da Vinci and Michelangelo. What other city

GUICCIARDINI.

in the world, save Athens, possesses such a glorious galaxy of genius?

The statue in this portico, representing Benvenuto holding the miniature model of his Perseus, recalls the half-pathetic, half-humorous account which he himself gives of the casting of his masterpiece. The excitement attending it had made him ill, and he was obliged to take to his bed during the all-important process, leaving his workmen to complete the task. As he lay tossing in a burning fever, a man whose body, he says, was as crooked as the letter "s," entered the room, and said in a sepulchral voice, "Oh, Benvenuto! your work is ruined past earthly remedy." "When I heard the words of this wretch," says Benvenuto, "I uttered a shriek which

BENVENUTO CELLINI.

might have been heard in the infernal regions, rose from my bed, and hurried on my clothes, giving kicks and blows to all who came near me." He then rushed to the furnace, encouraged the workmen, and at last, after tremendous exertions, saw that the mold was filled; whereupon he ate a hearty meal with his assistants, went to bed again with a light heart, and slept as sweetly as if he had never been ill in his life. The portrait of Benvenuto Cellini, painted when he was advanced in years, would seem to indicate a good old man, wrinkled with age and care, approach-

BENVENUTO CELLINI IN OLD AGE.

ing the end of a well-spent life. But Benvenuto was no saint, nor was his life a tranquil one. On the contrary, it was so full of reckless adventure that his own account of it reads like a romance. Rash, boastful and immoral, he handled a sword as skillfully as a chisel, and his career was marked by continual quarrels and not a few assassinations, — for which, however, he usually obtained prompt pardon on account of his won-

derful genius. At the same time there was another side to his character. It is to be remembered to his credit that he took into his house his widowed sister and her six children, and supported them with the greatest kindness.

The only way to retain agreeable memories of a vast gallery, like the Uffizi, is to pay it several visits and invariably seek the open air the instant that one feels fatigued. It is unfortunate that travelers do not always follow this simple rule; for, surely, it is a thousand times better to see, enjoy, and recollect a few choice masterpieces, than to gaze on and

on, till one is forced to retire with senses too fatigued to think of anything save physical exhaustion. Especially is this true in Florence, where, in the galleries of the Pitti and Uffizi, which are connected by a covered passageway and bridge, the tourist can walk for several miles through an unbroken series of long corridors and spacious rooms, the walls of which are lined with paintings or adorned with statues.

NICCOLA PISANO.

For those who insist on "doing" both museums in a single visit, electric tram-cars should be run from one end to the other. Some of the most unhappy-looking persons I have ever seen, I encountered in the Pitti and Uffizi. They should have been supremely happy there; but, on the contrary, they were limping wearily and reluctantly from room to room, as if they were going to a dentist's chair. " An art museum," said a connoisseur to me one day, " is like an artichoke; it should be enjoyed, leaf by leaf."

THE VENUS DI MEDICI.

The apartment of greatest value in the Uffizi is a small octagonal room called the Tribune. No single room of any gallery in the world contains so many masterpieces as this. Its walls are hung with works of Titian, Raphael, Michelangelo, Paul Veronese, Fra Bartolommeo, Domenichino, Guido Reni, and Correggio; and alternating with their wealth of color are five of the most famous gems of ancient sculpture, including the Interlocked Wrestlers and the Venus di Medici. Moreover, the room itself is worthy of its contents; since, with its cupola encrusted with mother-of-pearl, its gilded ceiling, mural decorations, and mosaic pavement, the apartment alone cost nearly one hundred thousand dollars.

THE NIOBE ROOM.

The traveler's first impression on beholding the Medici
Venus is, usually, that of disappointment. The surface of the
statue is, of course, imperfect; for, when discovered, it was
broken into eleven pieces, and had undoubtedly been buried in
the earth for centuries beneath the ruined mass of Hadrian's
Villa. These broken portions, it is true, have been well ad-

A CORNER IN THE NIOBE ROOM.

justed; but nothing can conceal the lines of jointure, or hide
the slight discolorations caused by long exposure to the soil.
Then, too, mankind has praised this work so lavishly, that it
almost invites unfriendly criticism; for in respect to works of
art, as well as to individuals, a host of people are made hostile
critics from the motive which impelled the old Athenian to
vote against Aristides, merely because he was tired of hearing him called "The Just." "Would you make me speak

ill of my friend?" asks La Rochefoucauld; "then speak, yourself, too highly in his praise."

Repeated visits to this statue, however, gradually dispelled my disappointment, till I became at last a genuine admirer of its immortal beauty. The marks of restoration, it is true, are visible; but what a proof it is of the perfection of this Venus that, although mutilated, she could at once resume her sovereignty when her dissevered members had been united, and that

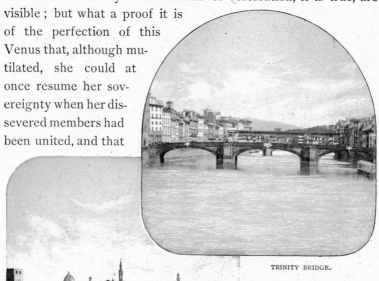

TRINITY BRIDGE.

THE ARNO.

she is still able to reveal the sculptor's thought expressed two thousand years ago! Oh, the sweetness and sadness of thinking of the millions who have gazed upon a work of art like this, and felt the same emotions that we feel, yet whom the senseless marble has outlived! The thousands of antiquity, who came to it, admired it and disappeared, leaving as little record in the world as last year's fallen leaves; and, then, the thousands of more recent times, — the artists, authors, poets, travelers, and friends whose work or love has influenced

our lives, — all of whom rendered homage to this deity, and
have since then in many instances passed away from earth,
while the fair statue still remains and smiles upon us calmly
in its sculptured loveliness, as it will doubtless smile on generations yet unborn. How many men and women, when they
stand before it with the glow of health upon their cheeks,
think of this figure with a kind of pity as being old! But
it survives them all, although so frail that a fanatic's blow
might ruin it, or even a missile thrown by a child's hand could
mar its loveliness forever.

Reaching the terminus of the Uffizi Portico, I found myself
on the Lung' Arno, a handsome street, which, as the name
denotes, borders the river for a considerable distance. What
the Seine is to Paris the Arno is to Florence. It divides the
city into well-nigh equal parts, and sweeps along beneath historic bridges and between huge granite walls. The need of
parapets to curb the torrent's violence was often felt in the
early history of the city. In 1557, for example, the Arno rose
to such a height that the contents of the shops were swept away
by the invading water, and even the roofs of the houses on the

ON THE LUNG' ARNO.

Ponte Vecchio were carried off by the impetuous current. Yet, notwithstanding its occasional caprices, the Florentines love their river, which is to them a source of great prosperity, since it furnishes an easy means of transportation to the sea.

It was the hour of noon when I arrived on the Lung' Arno, the very time when one would naturally expect to see some business traffic here; and yet its sidewalks were deserted. The reason was apparent; for the sun's rays were pouring so relentlessly upon the shadeless pavement, that the people had prudently retired into their houses or to the narrow streets. The hour of noon is, therefore, in hot weather the time of greatest silence in the Tuscan capital; for nothing but the ardent sun can dry to inarticulate repose the vocal chords of noisy Florentines.

Wherever shade prevails, however, Florence is usually a Bedlam. Street-venders call their wares with lusty lungs, and make the walls reverberate with their peculiar cries; and where most other people hum or whistle as they work, the merry Florentines prefer to sing. I once approached, on the Lung' Arno, a hackman who was so absorbed in rendering an air

TRINITY SQUARE.

THE CASINO ON A GALA DAY.

from "Il Trova-
tore" that he con-
tinued, quite in-
different to my
presence, till he
had finished the
refrain ; then, dis-
arming me with
an engaging smile,
he asked, "How
could I cut short
that fine aria,
signore ? "

Some years
ago, an artist
friend in Florence

THE STROZZI PALACE.

told me that a few nights before, three or four members of a
theatre orchestra had amused themselves by playing a waltz on
their violins and flutes as they walked homeward through the
streets. A crowd of Florentines quickly assembled, and followed
them dancing to the music. Where women could not be obtained
as partners, the men danced with each other as far as the residence of the last musician. When he had, finally, disappeared
within his house, the waltzers strolled back, arm in arm, singing
the air to which they had been dancing.

I greatly admire the mediæval palaces of Florence. They
look magnificently stern and warlike in their panoply of rough-
hewn stone, and are haunted by as many tragic memories as
there are granite blocks in their massive walls. For in the
days when Dante compared the Florentine Republic to a sick
man, who is constantly changing his position without ever
finding rest, these monumental palaces were domestic citadels,
within which several generations of the rival families of Florence, with their armed retainers, could withstand a siege ;

when, either as Guelfs or Ghibellines, they carried on the end-
less feuds which stained the streets so frequently with blood.
Their age alone would invest these structures with remarkable
interest. Thus, the Strozzi Palace had been completed and
occupied by Cosimo de' Medici before the discovery of America.
Even its ornaments are reminders of the olden time; for, in
the iron hoops, still visible beside the windows, banners waved
by day and torches burned at night for centuries; and nearer
to the base of the great structure are larger rings, to which
the horses of visitors were fastened; for Florentine nobles then
rode through the streets on horseback, not in carriages.

Quite different from its mediæval palaces, yet thoroughly
characteristic of Florence, are some old frescoed structures
near the Arno. Poor shabby dwellings they now are, reminding me of beggars clad in cast-off finery; and yet a charming
fresco here and there smiles through the grime of years, as in
the costume of a mendicant a piece or two may still remain
unfaded and unstained. Sometimes, on the edge of evening,
when their façades are gilded by the setting sun, they look

COURTYARD OF THE PALAZZO RICARDI.

OLD FRESCOED BUILDINGS.

like rare old tapestry, and hint of what they must have been;
as a bright smile or look of tenderness on the oldest and most
wrinkled face may give an instantaneous revelation of its former
beauty.   Who is it that says the only trump-card old people
have left is cheerfulness?

A love for frescoed walls is common to northern Italy.
I shall not soon forget a small hotel at which I stopped, on
my way to Florence, almost within the shadow of the Alps.
Its walls appeared to be alive with gaily colored gods,
goddesses, men, women, children, and animals at which the
peasants stared in open-mouthed admiration.   It was dark
when I arrived, and I saw nothing that night of the brilliant
hues; but I can still remember how comical it seemed next
morning, on looking out of my window, to see (so near that
I could touch them with my hand) the enormous figures of

THE DEMIDOFF MONUMENT.

two Alpine lovers, plighting their troth, in all the colors of the spectrum, on the exterior of my bedroom wall.

In a Florentine street where I resided for some time, I often passed a handsome monument erected to Prince Demidoff. The story of the man whom it commemorates is quite romantic. Although himself a Russian noble of enormous wealth, his father had been merely a village blacksmith, whose only fortune was a sturdy frame and a brave heart. Peter the Great, one day, in passing his shop, requested him to repair his carriage; and, as he watched him work, was greatly impressed with his extraordinary strength. Pleased, also, with his intelligent conversation the Tsar conceived the idea that Demidoff's mental capabilities might, possibly, be equal to his vigorous physique. Accordingly he placed him at the head of a new manufactory of firearms. Demidoff made it a magnificent success, and in ten years the Tsar presented him not only with a title of nobility, but, better still, with a Siberian estate on which some gold mines were discovered. The rest is easily imagined, save the unusual fact that the blacksmith's son, far from being ruined by his vast inheritance, became famous for his benevolence, and on his annual visits to Italy always gave to the poor of Florence the sum of forty thousand dollars.

Of all historic cities Florence is the brightest and most

cheerful in appearance. Venice, Rome, Constantinople, Cordova, and Athens impress the traveler with a sentiment of sadness. But Florence seems to possess the secret of perpetual youth. Her ancient edifices are not ruins. While other towns of Italy suggest the past in marks of desolation and decay, she bears the imprint of antiquity exquisitely graven on her brow like an intaglio. She has, apparently, made Time her lover, and for her sake he leaves his usual occupation of destruction, and even beautifies her stately buildings, notwithstanding their advancing years, as if, indeed, he knew that, were they once destroyed, Earth would wear nothing half so fair upon her breast. Thus, her superb Duomo is not seriously darkened, like most northern shrines; nor has the stern Palazzo Vecchio lost its rugged strength in battling with the storms of centuries; and the three hundred years that have elapsed since Giotto's tower was completed, have only given it a deeper loveliness,

PANORAMA OF FLORENCE

THE COURTYARD OF THE BARGELLO.

and its rich marble surface has even a more mellow tint than when it first rose sunward from the square.

Strolling one day through this enchanting city, still so fresh and beautiful, I stepped within the pictur-esque courtyard of the old Bargello, the residence of the Podestàs or criminal magistrates of Florence, who were invariably foreigners, because, in those fierce days of rival and contending factions, it was believed that strangers would ad-minister justice more impartially than citi-zens. Standing in this historic edifice I felt as if I had been sud-denly transported to the time of Dante. The ponderous arches, rich with sculpture, are the same that echoed to the footsteps of the ancient Flor-entines; and, as I walked among the columns, still adorned with rings for torches,

THE STAIRCASE.

hooks for lanterns and various sculptured decorations, so vivid was my realization of the history of Florence, that I could almost fancy the ghosts of Dante or Cellini to be lurking here amid the shadows. Yet how tragic are the memories which haunt these ancient palaces of Florence! With all its intellectual and artistic brilliancy, it was a place of almost incredible violence and cruelty. Thus, at the well in the centre of this courtyard many illustrious Florentines have been beheaded, and in a neighboring cell we may see the spot where a poor wretch was chained to the wall by an iron collar for thirty years. Here, too, in 1343, occurred one of the most appalling deeds in Florentine history. The Podestà had been besieged for weeks in the Bargello by members of the Medici and

THE ARMORY.

other families, who were determined that his tyranny should end. Finally, forced by starvation to capitulate, he agreed if his own life were spared to give up to their fury the principal agents of his cruelty, — a father and his son, the latter a lad but eighteen years of age. Shrieking for mercy, the wretched man and boy were thrust out through a door and over a railing into the court below, where the exasperated populace tore them limb from limb and, subsequently, bore the hideous fragments of their bodies through the streets upon the points of lances, — and this was done in Florence in the time of Dante! How true it is that a period of literary and artistic excellence is not of necessity an age of virtue or nobility of character!

Climbing the ancient staircase, up which so many had preceded us, we entered one of the halls of the Bargello. At present, the building is neither a palace nor a prison for state criminals, as was the case in the sixteenth century, but serves as a most interesting National Museum. Among a multitude of antique bronzes here displayed, the traveler turns to one,

THE MUSEUM OF THE BARGELLO.

as to an old and highly prized acquaintance. It is the Wingèd Mercury of John of Bologna. What an unfailing source of pleasure this inimitably graceful figure is! Even the poorest model that we see of it cannot completely lose the spirit of exultant energy and swift activity breathed into it by its creator. It is the ideal embodiment of fleetness and irrepressible youthful vigor. The sense of rapid movement through illimitable space that sometimes comes to us in dreams, finds its supreme expression in this messenger of the gods who spurns the earth with wingèd foot, impatient of delay. Yet though his progress is arrested, he has the absolute repose of perfect art, and causes us no restlessness because his flight is thus delayed. Monarch of motion, he stands serenely poised in an expectant attitude, which needs but the dissolving of some subtile spell to send him springing forward on his joyous mission.

Leaving this National Museum, as I was passing through one of the oldest and narrowest streets of Florence, I saw above the doorway of a tall stone house a marble tablet. Approaching it, I read with interest the words : " In this house, in 1265, was born the divine poet, Dante." The structure has been recently rebuilt, and almost ruined as a genuine relic of antiquity, but interest in the site it occupies can never die ; for, aside from its association with the author of the " Divine Comedy," it became, two hundred years after Dante's death, a kind of club where statesmen, artists, wits, and scholars loved to congregate, among them being Michelangelo and Benvenuto Cellini.

The tablet on the house of Dante is by no

THE WINGÈD MERCURY.

means an exception here. Florence shows the love she cherishes for her illustrious children by marking with inscriptions the historic buildings which have been illumined by their genius. Accordingly, the glory of antiquity greets us continually, and almost all the bridges, streets, and stately edifices of this Tuscan city have

DANTE'S HOUSE.

some associations with great men or deeds that thrill us by their
stirring memories.

> " 'Tis the Past
> Contending with the Present; and in turn
> Each has the mastery."

In the Via Ghibellina stands the house of Michelangelo,
which, as recently as 1858, was still owned by one of his descend-

DANTE.

ants, who then be-
queathed it to the
city of Florence. It
is intensely interest-
ing, because it brings
us nearer to the
human side of the
great genius than his
Titanic works can
ever do. So forceful,
grand, and awe-in-
spiring are his colossal
statues and frescos,
that their creator
seems at times almost
a demigod; and it is,
therefore, with a feel-
ing of relief that we
here see and touch,
in addition to the
easel, palette, and
brushes of the artist,
the armchair, walk-
ing-stick, and slippers
of the man.

The bust of Mi-
chelangelo, in the

THE HOUSE OF MICHELANGELO.

National Museum of Florence, reveals a face upon which thought, care, pain, and bitter struggles with the world have left deep traces ; a face, too, which had been disfigured for life by the blow of his envious fellow-student, Torregiano. Yet it is kindly, notwithstanding its severity and sadness ; and although its features are those of the cold and reserved sculptor, before whose gray hairs even Pope Julius II. rose in reverence, and in whose presence the Grand Duke Cosimo stood with uncovered head, they are also the lineaments of the man who nursed his aged servant in sickness with the tenderness of a mother and slept, without undressing, upon a couch that he might be ever near to render him assistance.

One of the most peculiar works of art in Florence is the mask of a satyr, carved by Michelangelo when a boy fifteen years of age. Lorenzo the Magnificent, who then governed Florence, was a great lover

MASK OF A SATYR. (*Michelangelo.*)

MICHELANGELO " PAUSING."

of art as well as a patron of painters, sculptors, and architects. Among the youth who came to study sculpture, in the school which had been founded by the Medici in Florence, was Michelangelo; and after a few days of application, this precocious lad had the courage to attempt to copy a faun's head in marble, and was so successful that Lorenzo was greatly impressed with his ability. He took occasion, however, to remind the lad that his faun was old and that aged people rarely have mouths well filled with teeth. Young Michelangelo immediately acted on the Prince's suggestion, breaking out two or three teeth, and indenting the jaw in such a way as to make the loss appear entirely natural. Next day Lorenzo, pleased at the youthful sculptor's quick appreciation of his criticism, in-

FLORENCE AND THE ARNO.

vited him to his palace, treated him like one of his own children, and gave him every opportunity to progress in his chosen profession.

A modern sculptor has represented Michelangelo as if pausing a moment from impetuous toil. Yet we are sure that the great master did not pause long at any time. In one of his letters occur the words, "It is only well with me, when I hold the chisel in my hand." He meant by this, undoubtedly, that then alone could he forget his individual sorrows and the misfortunes of his country; for he had learned that the busiest existence is the least unhappy, and that the true science of living is knowing how to fill the void in life with useful occupation. Even when more than sixty years of age, he would attack the marble with such fury as to make an ordinary sculptor catch his breath; and it is said that in fifteen minutes Michelangelo would strike off more pieces than three young stone-cutters could hew in thrice the time. In fact, the sight of a block of marble often awoke in him a fever of excitement; for, teeming with possibilities, it seemed to him to be a kind of prison, confining an idea which waited

THE CHURCH OF SAN LORENZO.

to be set at liberty by him. In one of his sonnets, addressed to
Vittoria Colonna, the noble woman whom he loved, he well
expressed this sentiment:

"As when, oh, lady mine, with chiseled touch,
    The stone unhewn and cold
    Becomes a living mold,
The more the marble wastes, the more the statue grows;
So, if the working of my soul be such,
That good is but evolved by Time's dread blows,
    The vile shell, day by day,
    Falls like superfluous flesh away;
Oh! take whatever bonds my spirit knows,
And reason, virtue, power, within me lay."

No visitor to Florence fails to see those wonderful productions of Michelangelo's genius in the sacristy of the Church
of San Lorenzo, — the tombs of Lorenzo and Julian de' Medici.
To comprehend the colossal figures which recline on these sar-
cophagi, one must understand something of the man who called
them into being. No other sculptor who has ever lived could
have created them. The intellectual and moral nature of this
lonely, contemplative man revealed itself in marble, as Shakespeare's genius showed itself in words. The recumbent statues

THE TOMB OF JULIAN DE' MEDICI.

THE TOMB OF LORENZO DE' MEDICI.

of Day and Night, Twilight and Dawn, were not intended to be beautiful; they are, however, Titanic, superhuman, and terrible, like the forces of Nature. One knows in looking at them that Michelangelo must have suffered. Thus, Dawn, as portrayed by him, is not a lovely maiden, joyously awakening to a day of happiness and love, but a mature woman whose brow is knit with pain, as if arising wearily to resume a hopeless task. Twilight, on the contrary, her male companion, yields willingly to an inclination to repose. The colossal statue of Day remains unfinished; but though the face is only roughly sketched, tremendous strength is visible, peering through the film of marble, like the sun struggling to pierce the clouds. Night seems the happiest of all, lying unconscious in a dreamless sleep. That this profoundly sad interpretation of the meaning of these figures is correct would seem to be proven by the oft-quoted lines written by the sculptor himself in reference to the statue of Night. Giovanni Strozzi, entering the sacristy one day during the absence of Michelangelo, had traced upon the wall lines which may be translated:

> "The Night which here thou seest thus sweetly sleeping,
> Was by an angel carved in this pure stone;
> Because she sleeps, she is alive;
> Awake her, if thou doubtest; she will speak to thee."

On reading this, Michelangelo replied in words which show the melancholy which the oppressed condition of his country then inspired:

> "Welcome to me is sleep, and still more so
> Is to be made of stone in these dark days
> Of shame and wrong. Not to perceive or feel
> Is joy to me. So wake me not. Speak low."

The statues of the Medicean princes, Lorenzo and Julian, are not portraits, and Michelangelo seems to have made no effort to produce their likenesses; for he remarked, "Who will appear a thousand years from now to prove that they looked otherwise?" The truth is, neither of them merited such a monument, nor ever had in life either the manly vigor or the intellectual force which these magnificent figures so effectually display. There are few statues in the world more interesting and suggestive than that of Lorenzo, which from its meditative attitude, with drooping head and the forefinger pressed upon the lip, has been sometimes called

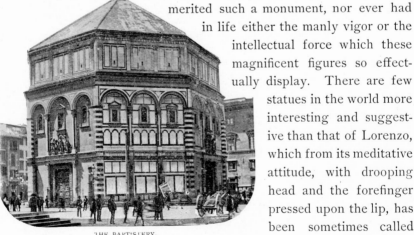

THE BAPTISTERY.

"*Il Pensiero*," "The
Thinker," and some-
times "The Thought
of Michelangelo." No
more expressive head
than this was ever
chiseled. It is that
of a strong man who
has endured suffering.
We feel instinctively
from something in his
face and posture that
he is not meditating
an act of cruelty.
There is a tender

GHIBERTI'S GATES.

heart behind the cold exterior. Yet, though it does not indicate
a man advanced in years, the statue is of one who has lived
much and has no more illusions. "He who has passed through
the door of disillusion," it is said, "has died twice." Whatever be the number of his years, such a man is really old. For
him who hopes and believes, there is a future; for him who
has lost hope and faith, there is only a past. One anticipates,
the other remembers.

One of the oldest and most interesting structures in Florence
is the Baptistery, which, though comparatively small, was originally the cathedral of the city. The erection of the grand
Duomo near it has not robbed it of its usefulness, for at its
font, even now, all the children born in Florence are baptized.
In point of art, too, the Baptistery, though far more modest in
appearance than the adjoining Campanile and Cathedral, is
inexpressibly rich in the possession of a series of bronze doors
which have elicited for centuries the admiration of the world.
These wonderful portals by Andrea Pisano and Ghiberti, with
their elaborate panels filled with life-like figures, would of

themselves make Florence famous; and when Andrea's were
completed, the Senators of the Republic, who never left the
Palazzo Vecchio together except for the most important ceremonies, came in a body to behold them, and to bestow distinguished honors upon the artist who had labored on them forty
years.   Even more significant and enduring was the praise
bestowed upon Ghiberti's masterpiece by Michelangelo, a
hundred years later, when he exclaimed, "They are worthy to
be the gates of Paradise."   Words are fleeting, it is said, but
this eulogy pronounced by the greatest artist of the modern
world may, possibly, outlast the bronze gates which inspired it.

Standing in close proximity to the Baptistery is the most
conspicuous feature of the Tuscan capital — the first to greet us
on approaching Florence, the last to linger in our vision as we
take our leave — its world-renowned cathedral.   Crowned with the
glorious dome of Brunelleschi, and sheathed from street to roof
with blocks of variegated marble and adorned with countless
specimens of artistic sculpture, the noble edifice rises in majestic
beauty from the centre of the city, like a stupendous mountain
of Florentine mosaic.   Viewed from the hills encircling Flor-

THE CATHEDRAL.

ence, the other build-
ings seem to cluster
about this structure
as soldiers gather
round a standard
elevated in the sight
of all. What a con-
ception of the noble
spirit of the early
Florentines we gain
by reading the de-
cree which, in 1294,
ordered Arnolfo, the
first of the cathe-
dral's architects, "to

EXTERIOR OF THE CATHEDRAL.

raise the loftiest, most sumptuous, and most magnificent pile
that human invention could devise and human labor execute"!
Succeeding generations for six hundred years have carved their
epitaphs upon its mass, as coral insects leave their skeletons in

the reefs they
build; and every
stone within its
walls bears wit-
ness to the grand
ideals or sublime
achievements of
Brunelleschi,
Donatello, Giotto,
and scores of their
contemporaries or
followers, whose
names have won
an immortality of
fame.

A CORNER OF THE CATHEDRAL.

Superior even to the walls of this cathedral, encrusted though they are with marble panels, is the especial glory of the edifice, — its matchless dome. The creation of this by Brunelleschi marked an epoch in the history of architecture. As the huge framework of the noble edifice climbed slowly heavenward, it was perceived that the construction of a dome, to span the gulf which yawned between its lofty walls, would be supremely difficult.   In fact, no dome of such dimensions had

then been at-tempted since the completion of the Pantheon at Rome, before the birth of Christ; and even the Pan-theon's majestic cupola rested on walls but seventy-two feet high, while those of this cathedral were one hundred and thirty feet in alti-tude.   But Bru-nelleschi solved

THE DOORWAY.

the difficult problem, and made a model which he submitted to the judges.   How confident he was that he alone was master of the situation is shown by his suggestion that artists from all parts of Italy, France, and Germany be invited to compete with him, and by the fact that during the discussion of their relative merits he left Florence for Rome, and remained there until he was entreated to return.

At last, in 1420, before a concourse of artists and architects, Brunelleschi proposed his plan of erecting a double dome, one inside the other, leaving a space between the two. When his astonished auditors inquired how this could be done, he is said to have resorted to the device adopted seventy years later by Columbus. Calling for an egg he requested any one present to make it stand on end. When each in turn declined, Brunelleschi broke the shell of the egg sufficiently to make a broadened base for its support; and when all declared they could have done as much, the architect replied that they would no doubt be able, also, to build the dome were he to explain to them his method. Brunelleschi was appointed architect, and the result abundantly justified the selection; for, when the enormous void was vaulted over by a dome which rose in grand simplicity, and stood aloft without apparent support, the fame of its designer was secure forever.

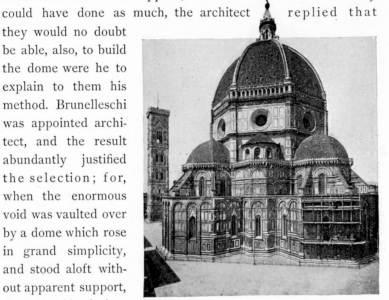

THE CATHEDRAL DOME.

With the exception of the cupola of St. Peter's, the dimensions of which are a trifle larger, this is the most majestic dome that man has ever reared. Other great domes, like those of the Pantheon at Rome, and Santa Sophia at Constantinople, were designed principally for their interior effect; but the creation of Brunelleschi, while grand within, is even more imposing from without. One hardly realizes at first its gigantic size, so perfect is its symmetry, and so harmonious with the rest of the cathedral are its vast proportions; but the marble lantern on its

BRUNELLESCHI.

summit, which looks like a small chapel on a mountain crest, is really more than seventy feet in height, and would itself form, on the level earth, a building of considerable size. A sentence uttered by Michelangelo in reference to this dome, more than a century after its completion, forms an appropriate pendant for his famous eulogy of Ghiberti's gates. Every one knows how greatly he admired this work of Brunelleschi, and how, on leaving Tuscany for Rome, there to become the architect of St. Peter's, he looked back tenderly at the serene and noble outline of this crown of Florence, and exclaimed:

> "*Io farò la sorella*
> *Piu grande già, ma non più bella.*"

> "I will make her sister
> Larger indeed, but not more beautiful."

Although the Florentine cathedral was opened for religious worship, and was consecrated by the Pope in person on the 25th of May, 1436, its beautiful façade was not completed until 1887. The unveiling of this was an occasion of great rejoicing throughout Italy. Deputations from all the principal Italian cities were in attendance, and the impressive ceremony was presided over by the King and Queen. An immense curtain had been drawn from the base to the summit of the façade and,

finally, at a signal given by the King, who with his royal con-
sort was seated on a platform opposite the cathedral, this was
slowly lowered.   The result was far more effective than it
would have been had the curtain been raised; for, as the snow-
white screen descended, the impression was produced of a
beautiful marble temple emerging from a cloud.   For several
minutes the multitude of spectators stood in perfect silence,
completely spellbound by an overpowering sense of beauty;
then, from ten thousand voices, came a storm of cheers and
acclamations, and Queen Margherita was so deeply moved
that, bowing her head, she burst into tears.

In harmony with the rest of the edifice, the entire front of
the Duomo rises before the spectator like a splendid screen
of marble marquetry, adorned with sculptured flowers, fruits,
and garlands, among which stands its population of white-robed
prophets, saints, and angels poised upon delicately chiseled
pinnacles, ensconced in niches lined with rich mosaic, or clinging still more closely to the walls in bas-reliefs.

There was a political, as well as historical, significance in
the completion of this façade.   When Victor
Emmanuel had been proclaimed King of
united Italy, the Florentines received a
promise that their city should become,
eventually, the capital of the nation.
The promise was fulfilled and, from
1865 till 1871, the Pitti Palace was
the residence of the King, and
Florence was the capital of Italy.
As a result, its citizens made many
changes, and incurred expenses which
they would never have assumed had
they supposed that, six years later, the
Court would be removed to Rome; and
it was to recompense them for their losses

QUEEN MARGHERITA.

THE FRONT OF THE CATHEDRAL.

and bitter disappointment, that the Florentines were then assured the chief edifice of their city should no longer remain unfinished.

It is not surprising, therefore, that the Florentines who assisted at the crowning act in the construction of the Duomo were hardly less enthusiastic than those who laid its corner-stone. All the sculptors and artists who labored to produce it undertook it as a work of love, and many of them accepted for their services nothing but their actual expenses. Nor was this disinterestedness limited to the army of laborers. Much of the variegated marble used in the construction of the splendid work was a gift, even the cost of its transportation being paid by the contributors. For, as Browning said,

THE DUOMO, AND THE CAMPANILE.

"Open my heart, and you will see
Graven inside of it, Italy."

So in the heart of Florence lies her idolized Duomo.

The Campanile of Giotto, which rises close beside the Florentine Duomo, is universally conceded to be one of the most perfect and beautiful structures in the world. It is difficult to speak of it without the appearance of exaggeration, and equally impossible to overstate its beauty. Although quadrangular, massive, and nearly three hundred feet in height, it is yet as delicate and graceful as a stately flower. Rising in five stories, each loftier than the one beneath it, it is entirely composed of variegated marble, and its whole surface is adorned

THE CAMPANILE.

with exquisitely pointed windows, slender columns, elaborate
statues and reliefs, together with innumerable minor sculptured
decorations.   It is not strange, then, that citizens of Florence,
when they can find
no adequate expres-
sion for some lovely
object, will say, as
if they thus attained
the climax of com-
parison, "It is as
beautiful as the Cam-
panile."

GIOTTO.

The career of
Giotto, the Floren-
tine sculptor, painter,
and architect is, per-
haps, the most strik-
ing proof of the fact
that in an age of in-
tellectual fertility
genius appears to
spring miraculously
from a hitherto un-
cultivated soil.   The
painter Cimabue
found him, a boy of
ten years, drawing
upon a piece of slate
one of the sheep
which he was tend-
ing, and, struck with his dawning talent, took him as a
pupil.   The result was marvelous.   Giotto not only originated
and executed a great variety of beautiful frescos, but it
was he who covered much of the exterior of the cathedral

THE PONTE VECCHIO.

with its splendid mantle, and built its unrivaled bell-tower, —a model for all time.

The Baptistery, Campanile, and Cathedral form an architectural trio worthy of the Golden Age of Florence. None of them would suffice without the others; but together they reveal to us the best artistic and religious aspirations of her citizens: the Baptistery, at whose sacred font the dawning life of every Florentine receives its consecration; the Duomo, whose gigan-

tic roof arches above him as he kneels in prayer; and the ethereal Campanile, pointing heavenward as if reminding him of immortality. These three together symbolize the trilogy of human history, —birth, life, and death.

The Ponte Vecchio is not

ARCHES OF THE PONTE VECCHIO.

only the oldest of the six bridges which cross the Arno, it is also the most picturesque. Unlike all other bridges I have ever seen, it has two thoroughfares (one above the other) and a line of small windows in the upper story denotes a section of the long and winding passageway, built to connect the Palace of the Uffizi on one side of the river with the Pitti Palace on the other. Even the lower story is, also, enclosed save in the centre, where a pretty portico, with three graceful arches, affords delightful views up and down the stream. Clinging to the sides of the old structure, as they have done for centuries, are numerous shops of jewelers and goldsmiths, in one of which, three hundred years ago, worked Benvenuto Cellini. The sight of this old bridge is sufficient to recall most of the great events in Florentine history; for it was built, in 1362, by Taddeo Gaddi; and, doubtless, every famous citizen of Florence, in the intervening centuries, often crossed it and, leaning on the parapet of its loggia, gazed upon substantially the same view that greets the visitor to-day. Nor has literature failed to impart to it the charm of romance; for, in George Eliot's novel, "Romola," it was from the arches of this Ponte Vecchio that Tito, to escape the mob, leaped into the river, to swim with the descending current to the open country, where, as he landed in exhaustion, he met the fate he had deserved, — death by the hands of the old man he had betrayed.

One of the glories of Florence is the Pitti Palace, the residence of the King and Queen when Florence was the capital of united Italy. How thoroughly characteristic of old Florence, with its feuds and factions, was the idea to which this building owes its origin! Four hundred years ago a Florentine noble by the name of Luca Pitti was envious of the splendid

THE PITTI PALACE.

dwelling of his rival, the Strozzi. Accordingly he summoned Brunelleschi, whose construction of the cathedral's dome had given him a rank among the first of architects, and begged him to create for him a palace, the mere courtyard of which should be large enough to contain the entire residence of the Strozzi. The next day Brunelleschi's plan was offered and accepted, for

A WINDOW IN THE PITTI PALACE.

he had designed an edifice with a courtyard, the dimensions of

THE PITTI PALACE, FROM THE REAR.

which exceeded that of the Strozzi mansion by three feet on each side. Pitti, however, ruined himself in the attempt to build it, and his magnificent abode passed finally into other hands, while that of the Strozzi is owned by their descendants to the present day.

The Pitti Palace is, nevertheless, a marvelous proof of the
solidity and strength of the architecture of that age; for,
during more than four hundred years, none of its massive
blocks of unhewn stone has had to be replaced, and there is
no apparent reason why it may not last four centuries more.
It is appropriate that a building which has so successfully
defied the touch of Time should be a treasure-house of Art.

Few European palaces can equal it in its number of fine
paintings,—to copy some of which an artist must make application five years in advance, so numerous are the petitioners
for the privilege. If every other gallery in the Old World,
save this, should be destroyed, Europe would still be rich.
Moreover, the decorations of the halls containing these pictures
make them worthy receptacles for the works themselves. The
lofty ceilings are covered with paintings framed in gold, and

DUPRÉ'S "CAIN" AND "ABEL."

VICTORY, IN THE PITTI.

THE ROOM OF THE " MADONNA OF THE CHAIR."

even the cornices are adorned with statues. On entering the Pitti, as you walk upon the exquisitely inlaid floors, put out your hand, and it may touch a table of mosaic, malachite, or lapis-lazuli, the cost of which was possibly a hundred thousand dollars; sit down to rest, and you will find yourself upon a chair of satin, silk brocade, or velvet; look around you in bewilderment, and you will see a multitude of walls on which, from gorgeous roof to sculptured marble dado, hang the world's great masterpieces. Even the doors through which you pass have frames of variegated marble, and you could make one visit here and feel yourself repaid without examining a single picture. It is easy, therefore, to believe the legend that when a prince of the Medici family lay dying in this palace, and an old priest endeavored to console him by telling him of mansions in the skies, the dying man exclaimed, " My father, however glorious they may be, I would be perfectly satisfied could I but remain in the Pitti."

Among the paintings in this palace is one before which every visitor must pause, though all the others be passed unnoticed. It is the sweetest and most tender of all Raphael's creations, — the " Madonna of the Chair." Aside from its religious significance, the instinct of humanity has been to treat this as the purest portraiture of motherhood that the world knows, and it would seem impossible for any one to look upon this group without a deeper reverence for the self-sacrificing tenderness that motherhood implies. No matter what may be the various nationalities of those who come and go before it, with reverent step and bated breath, a com- mon instinct of fraternity pervades them all. "One touch of Nature makes the whole world kin." In turn, the gorgeous palace van- ishes from each traveler's gaze, and in its place he sees his far-off home, feels once again the clasp of arms that, for his welfare, never knew fatigue ; and

THE " MADONNA OF THE CHAIR."

hears the voice which had a power to soothe all cares and griefs away, as nothing else, alas! can do. But, for a heart responsive to the religious influences of this work of art, it has a still more thrilling interest, representing the Divine Mother already seeing through the vista of the future, the anguish of Gethsemane and the tragedy of Calvary, and holding, therefore, the more closely to her breast the Child whose destiny already fills her with an exultant joy, behind which lurks a nameless dread.

The Boboli Gardens, adjoining the Pitti Palace, form a charming place of rest for those who have become wearied in the picture gallery. The glimpses of the city which their

stately avenues dis-
close are exquisitely
beautiful, and I recall
few more delightful
moments than those
which I have spent
here, sitting, book in
hand, within the
shade of cypress,
pine, and ilex trees,
or strolling through
a shadowy maze of
trellised pathways
framed in lofty
hedges, among which

THE BOBOLI GARDENS.

numerous statues are ensconced, their graceful figures gleaming white as snow against thick walls of living green.

It seems appropriate to find among the cypress trees of

STATUARY IN THE BOBOLI.

Florence the
forms of the
gods and god-
desses of Greek
mythology. It is
as if the deities
of the past,
homeless, and
excluded from
all modern
creeds, had
chosen to return
and linger in a
place where they
can realize that
they still exist in

half the poems, paintings, and statues of the world, and where so many relics of the genius of antiquity remind them of the art that made earth beautiful, when men and women worshiped them as real.

In a handsome square, before the celebrated Church of Santa Croce, stands an imposing statue of the poet Dante. Florence is proud enough of Dante now, and, "with the late remorse of love," desires to show the world that she reveres his memory. The inauguration of this statue, on the 12th of May, 1865, the six hundredth anniversary of the poet's birth, will never be forgotten in the history of Florence. The entire city was hung with flags and garlands, and quotations from the works of Dante were placed on all the bridges, monuments, and buildings which he had described. Beautiful banners, bearing appropriate inscriptions, had been sent hither from all parts of Italy, and these were carried in a grand procession, led by King Victor Emmanuel, in celebration of the Italian unity which had been dreamed of, and ardently cherished by, Dante, six centuries before. Conspicuous in this procession was the actress Ristori, symbolizing Tragedy, and wearing on her head a crown of gold; while beside her

DANTE'S STATUE, AND THE CHURCH OF SANTA CROCE.

MONUMENT TO LUIGI CHERUBINI.

walked those great Italian actors, Salvini and Rossi, each holding the ribbon of a banner representing Dramatic Art. Finally,
when the vast concourse of spectators had as-
sembled in this
square, the solemn
bell of the Palazzo
Vecchio ceased its
vibrations, and,
while inspiring
music filled the
air, Victor Em-
manuel gave the

THE TOMB OF MICHELANGELO.

signal for the unveiling of the statue. At Dante's feet is the
figure of an eagle. Appropriate, indeed, the king of birds
beside the king of bards!

The Church of Santa Croce is the Westminster Abbey of
Florence, — the recognized shrine of Italian genius. Here are
the tombs of Michelangelo, Galileo, and the poet Alfieri, who
said that his first wish to acquire fame awoke within his breast
while walking in the aisles of Santa Croce. Here, also, the
subtle brain of Machiavelli finally found rest; while other
tombs of prominence are those of Cherubini, the composer,
and Raffaello Morghen, the engraver. It is especially appropriate that Michelangelo should be buried here; for not only
was Florence the city of his love, but this particular spot in
Santa Croce was chosen by him as his place of sepulture; since

THE CENOTAPH OF DANTE.

from this place, when the doors of the church are open, one can look out on the magnificent dome of the cathedral which he so admired.

A most impressive feature of this edifice is the Cenotaph of Dante. Hoping to obtain his body from Ravenna, the Florentines erected this for its reception, but in vain, — the splendid sepulchre is tenantless. Yet there was justice in the answer of the Ravennese: "You exiled Dante when in life, and set a price upon his head. With us he found a home and grave; and here he shall remain forever." Under the circumstances, therefore, this monument seems a brand of shame upon the brow of Florence. It is, indeed, imposing, for all its figures are colossal. On one side, Poetry mourns her loss; while on the other, star-crowned Fame points upward to the statue of the bard, as though about to utter the quotation from the "Inferno," which appears on the sarcophagus, "*Onorate l'altissimo Poeta.*"

There is a burial-place in Florence, dearer by far to all American hearts in its simplicity than even the magnificent shrine of Santa Croce. It is the Protestant Cemetery. Its situation was formerly more beautiful than now, for the old

THE INTERIOR OF SANTA CROCE.

city walls which sheltered it have been removed, and modern
thoroughfares surround it.   In fact, on account of its circum-
scribed area, no more interments will be made, and a new
burial-ground has been provided in another part of the city.
But English and American visitors will always reverently come
to this, since in its hallowed precincts lies the precious dust of
authors, poets, artists, and travelers, whose fate it was to die
here, far from home.   Among them are Walter Savage Landor,
Arthur Hugh Clough, Mrs. Trollope, and Theodore Parker,
and (dearest of all, to thousands of her readers), England's
greatest poetess, Elizabeth Barrett Browning.   Her resting-
place is marked by a sarcophagus of pure white marble, bearing her initials, and, through the spring and summer months
red roses bloom, and lilies lift their snowy heads above her
silent heart.   Her poet-husband acted wisely in giving her a
burial-place in Florence rather than in England; for, partly
on account of her long residence here for the sake of her
health, and partly because of the birth of her child in Florence,
this city had become the idol of her heart.   The very air of

THE PROTESTANT CEMETERY.

Florence breathes of her presence, since almost every prominent portion of the city is associated with her by her glorious
verse; and in the house called " Casa Guidi " where she died,
in 1861, and at whose " windows " she so often wrote, a marble
tablet has been placed by grateful Florentines, stating with
truth that by her poetry she formed a golden link between
Italy and England.

Whether or not the name of Florence is derived from the

MRS. BROWNING'S TOMB.

Latin *Florentia*, the Tuscan capital has been for centuries ap-
propriately called the City of Flowers. A lily figures in the
Florentine coat of arms, and in the spring the hills environing
Florence are literally carpeted with lilies, violets, tulips, and
crocuses. Bouquets of roses, hyacinths, and carnations, also,
can then be bought here for a few pennies. In walking for
the first time through the streets of Florence, or driving in the
park, you will usually be approached by a pretty flower-girl,

who offers you with an engaging smile and a few words, in the most musical of languages, a beautiful bouquet. Even if you refuse to purchase, she will at least contrive to slip a nosegay into your hand or toss a bunch of roses into your carriage, and if you accept them, she considers you there-

IN THE GARDENS OF THE PITTI.

after her patron, and expects to keep you supplied with flowers during your sojourn in the city. For these she frequently accepts

A GATE IN THE BOBOLI GARDENS.

no pay whatever at the time, relying on your generosity, when you depart, to give her more than she would otherwise receive. Thanks to the floral paradise in which it lies, Florence in May is enchanting; and I know of no city on earth more thoroughly delightful than this, when her historic streets and squares are white with the splendor of the moon, and the perfume and fascination of springtime are over all. Florence, it is true, is always charming; but it is in the youth of the year that we can best appreciate

"The vines, the flowers, the air, the skies that fling
Such wild enchantment o'er Boccaccio's tales
Of Florence and the Arno."

The public park of Florence, known as the Cascine, is a delightful place in which to walk and drive, and corresponds to the Parisian Bois de Boulogne. In the afternoon, especially, it is the rendezvous for all the gay and fashionable life of the city, and near the Casino, where refreshments are served and music is furnished by a military band, the Florentine gentlemen come and go from carriage to carriage, making little social visits, as they are wont to do among the boxes at the opera. A singular feature of this park is the imposing and half-Oriental funeral monument of the Maharaja of Kolhapur, who died in Florence, in 1870,   and was cremated on the spot where the memorial stands.   Far more interesting and at-

THE MAHARAJA'S MONUMENT.

"UNDULATING HILLS."

tractive, however, than this promenade of fashion, are the other suburbs of Florence.

The city is surrounded by soft, undulating hills, dotted with white-walled castles and innumerable villas, and green with cypresses and olives. There is an indescribable charm for me in olive trees. They cannot be called graceful or symmetrical, but even when their trunks are twisted and decayed, they wear a crown of silvery foliage that makes them beautiful, and that for centuries has been regarded as the emblem of peace.

To drive or walk upon the hills surrounding Florence is a constant source of pleasure, not merely from the charming landscape thus disclosed, but from the fact that on these pretty slopes are houses which have formed the homes of men and women who have filled the world with their renown. Thus — not to mention the resi-

THE ARCH OF GALILEO.

dences once occupied by Lorenzo the Magnificent, Machiavelli
and Boccaccio — the Brownings lived for several seasons on
these heights, above the Tuscan city and its summer heat, extending hospitality to many friends; here Hawthorne spent
some months, while writing portions of the "Marble Faun";
the famous tenor, Mario, also, and his equally celebrated wife,
Giulia Grisi, made this their home for years; and here reside,
to-day, the novelist "Ouida" and the tragedian Salvini. Sev-

A FLORENTINE STUDIO.

eral American sculptors, too, have found upon these hills a
place of residence thoroughly congenial to their tastes and
work. Fortunate men! What more delightful and stimulating
mode of life can be imagined than that of a sculptor, living
on one of the terraces of this historic amphitheatre, steeped
in the glorious Italian sunshine, and drawing inspiration from
the classic and artistic atmosphere of Florence!

I have greatly enjoyed visiting the studios of artists in Flor-

ence, for I love to watch a painter or a
sculptor at his work. It has always
seemed to me, however, that sculpture in
clay must be more fascinating even than
painting. To cause lines of symmetry
and beauty to grow out of formless
earth; to see curve, dimple, and contour
appear as by the touch of an invisible
enchanter's wand; to be able by the
half-caressing imprint of the thumb or
finger to accentuate the arch of an eye-
brow, or to impart smiling, immortal
sweetness to motionless and silent lips;
to reproduce with tiny strokes expressions
borrowed from the face before him, the

THE VENUS OF CANOVA.

droop of an eyelid, the curve of a nostril, or the cleft in a stern
chin; to see likeness, all at once and as if by magic, spring out
of what was until then merely an uninteresting mass of clay;

THORVALDSEN.

to watch the concrete beauty of
the individual blossom out of the
abstract of the race; and, finally,
to realize the possession of creative
power, in having called into existence a shape which, but an hour
ago, was without form and void,
— surely this must be one of the
most divine of pleasures, linking
the sculptor, in a way, with his
Creator, and giving him a wonderful appreciation of the joy
which moved the morning stars
to sing together, when, far away
in the dawn of the universe, God
called the earth out of prime-

val chaos, and made from it the crowning act of His creation.

The eternal difference between the Master and His pupils is that the breath of life, the living soul, is the work of the former alone. Could the sculptor impart this to earth, he too would be divine. He most nearly achieves it, however, when, with his genius consecrated to the pure ideal of eternal truth, he throws into his work, not only his entire skill, but all the concentrated

A STUDIO, FLORENCE.

passion of his soul. Sculptors have told me that the very touch of clay was a pleasure to them, because it seems so perfectly responsive, and quickly becomes warm beneath their hands, as if about to tremble into life. To them the original plastic work is infinitely more enjoyable than all the rest, which is largely drudgery; and, quickened by their enthusiasm, I have been better able to understand the beautiful words of Thorwaldsen: "Clay is the birth; plaster the death; and marble the resurrection."

HALL OF HONOR, VINCIGLIATA.

Prominent among the structures on these Tuscan hills is the Castle of Vincigliata. A quarter of a century ago, it was a crumbling, mediæval fortress, utterly useless to its owner, and interesting to the public merely as a pleasant terminus for a walk or drive. One day, however, Mr. Temple Leader, an English gentleman of wealth and leisure, became so enamoured of the old ruin, that he immediately purchased and proceeded to restore it; and now, in the absence of its owner, the public

THE CASTLE OF VINCIGLIATA.

is admitted to enjoy its beauties. In response to our knock on the iron door, the custodian smilingly granted our request to enter, and led us into a superbly decorated courtyard. I looked about me with surprise, not that the purchaser had spent a large amount of money here (such eccentricities are not unknown), but that the restoration was so perfect as to challenge criticism. In fact, the guardian and ourselves appeared to be the sole anachronisms in the place; for the narrow windows, quaint medallions, arches, columns, and stone pavement told us, as books could never do, how life went on upon the Tuscan Apennines, when Dante wrote his immortal poem, and Brunelleschi planned his dome. This castle, how-ever, existed nearly three hundred years before the age of Dante, being mentioned in the annals of Florence as early as 1031. Not much is known of its history; but it probably did not differ materially from that of most of the mediæval fortresses of Europe, and, no doubt, furnished its full share of cruelty and bloodshed, as well as of chivalry and warlike exploits. At all events, perched on this hill eight hundred feet above the sea, it must have been a stronghold easily defended against attack.

We found an hour far too short a time in which properly to see and enjoy this building. It is not only a valuable museum of antiquities, but a most instructive object lesson in the life and customs of the Middle Ages, since every detail of decoration and construction has been worked out with absolute historic accuracy. Thus, the square points along the walls and towers indicate the form of architecture chosen by

THE ENTRANCE TO THE CASTLE.

THE CLOISTER.

the Guelfs to distinguish their structures from those of their rivals, — the Ghibellines. The walls of the cloister, too, are adorned with frescos representing prominent events connected with the castle's history; the rooms are enriched with valuable specimens of antique furniture; and even the kitchen has enormous cupboards and cooking-utensils in brass, such as were used in former centuries. The amount of stone-carving that ornaments the edifice is astonishing, and must have cost its artistic owner a small fortune. Thus, at almost every angle emerges an elaborately carved gargoyle; above each doorway is a statue; every column has a beautifully sculptured capital; the well, which supplies good water from a depth of two hundred and forty feet, has a richly decorated curb; and the adjoining walls have been adorned with carved heads, portions of Roman ruins, and the statues of saints. By a singular fancy of the owner, too, marble tablets have been inserted in the masonry of the courtyard to commemorate visits

paid to Vincigliata by distinguished people. Anywhere else in
the world, we should expect to see such souvenirs preserved in
the form of cards, or inscriptions in a Visitor's Book; but
in this land of sculpture they are recorded in enduring marble.
As we were taking our leave, the guardian of the building
pointed to a fresco representing St. Christopher. "Take a
good look at that," he said; "a glance at it will save you,
during the entire day, from the danger of sudden death! That

A CORNER OF THE LOGGIA OF VINCIGLIATA.

is why the master had it painted near the gateway, so that no
one who enters or leaves the castle can fail to see it."

Crowning a cypress-covered hill, three miles from Florence,
stands the old monastery of La Certosa, its white walls glistening
in the sun as they have done for more than five hundred years.
So far as a defensible site and massive construction are con-
cerned, it might survive as many centuries more, but now
its days are numbered; for, like many other monasteries in

LA CERTOSA.

Italy,   it has been   abolished by the government.
Yet, though the farm belonging
to the monks is leased by the
authorities for cultivation, the
government has consented, out
of pity for its worthy inmates,
to leave the monastery undisturbed, un-
til the few
brothers who
remain there
shall have
passed away.
A white-haired
monk, clad in

LA CERTOSA, AND CONVENT-YARD.

the pure white robe of the Order, received us courteously, and
led us into an enclosure, consisting of a spacious vegetable

and flower garden
surrounded by
long cloisters,
which have for
centuries echoed
to the footsteps
of Carthusian
monks. Only about
ten brothers are
now left, all of
them old, and
some too feeble to
do even the little
work of caring for
the cabbages and
roses. The monk
who acted as our

THE MONKS OF LA CERTOSA.

guide gave each of us a small bouquet, and offered for sale not only some of the famous cordial which they manufacture, but also cakes of soap and bottles of perfumery. How odd it seemed to think of these aged monks, awaiting death within their ancient monastery, yet thus providing for the comfort of the outside world, of which they know so little!

The Church of La Certosa is superb with its marble candelabra, numerous statues and ornaments of lapis-lazuli. Moreover, I have rarely seen, even in Spain, such elaborate wood-carving as that which decorates the stalls and wardrobes for the monks, and I have never walked upon a more magnificent pavement than that which here displays its glittering expanse of variegated marble, inlaid with beautiful designs of white, red, black, and green mosaic.

Though less gorgeously decorated than the church, the chapter-house of the monastery would repay a visit, if only to behold the recumbent statue of a former superior of the order, Leonardo Buonafede, which lies upon the marble floor, apparently sunk in a sleep that has continued for three hundred

THE COURT AND GARDEN OF LA CERTOSA.

and fifty
years. As a
specimen of
elaborate
workmanship
this figure has
few equals;
for, from the
exquisitely
embroidered
cushion which
supports the
bishop's head
to the rings on
his forefinger
and thumb,
and the stock-
ings on his
feet, every-
thing reveals
the most scru-
pulous atten-
tion to details.

INTERIOR OF THE CHURCH OF LA CERTOSA.

Despite my efforts to the contrary, I found myself, when
near this reminder of death, furtively looking at the venerable
monk who stood beside us, and picturing this little brotherhood
becoming gradually smaller and smaller, until at last but two
survivors should remain to gaze into each other's eyes, dread-
ing the hour when only one of them will be left — the last of
all in these deserted halls — to die. These sad reflections were,
however, quickly dispelled when, changing my position, I gained
a front view of the slumbering prelate. Involuntarily I laughed
aloud; for the head, inclined a little to one side, gives to the
statue a peculiarly jocose appearance, as if the worthy man

PLEASANT DREAMS.

were feigning sleep, and might at any moment open his eyes and laugh at us for our mistake. Such absolute satisfaction I have never seen depicted elsewhere in a sculptured face. Apparently his dreams are most agreeable. No midnight call to prayer disturbs him now. "After life's fitful fever he sleeps well." We may be sure that to the last he loved good cheer, and frequently assumed, just after dinner, the peaceful attitude which the shrewd sculptor deemed best suited to his memory. The cheerful influence of this statue so affected us, that all the gloomy thoughts suggested by the waning brotherhood vanished; and, ere we rode down from the mountain height, we made use of the excellent cordial manufactured here, to drink the toast that the remaining brothers might feel in life and show in death as much serene contentment as Buonafede.

Upon the hill of Bellosguardo, overlooking Florence and the valley of the Arno, stands a structure, which, although

GALILEO.

unpretending and weather-beaten, possesses an undying interest, as the place where Galileo read the secrets of the midnight
sky. A servant, old enough apparently to have assisted at the
astronomer's observations, answered our ring at the gate, and
led us through a court which echoed loudly to our footsteps,
as if protesting at the intrusion. A moment later we entered
the humble room where the illustrious scientist had lived and
labored. His writing-table stood in its accustomed place, his
marble bust looked down upon us from the corner, and near it
was the stair-
way leading
to the roof
on which he
spent so many
hours gazing
heavenward.
Upon the
wall, also, a
marble tablet
reminded us
that the eyes
of Galileo,
which had so
often scanned

HOUSE OF GALILEO.

the glories of the sky, were veiled to earth some years
before his death, and that he lived here totally blind, —
an affliction in its way as terrible to him as deafness was
to Beethoven. It was during the time that he was thus de-
prived of vision that, at the age of seventy-four, he received
the visit of Milton, who, as a young man of thirty, little
anticipated then that he would one day suffer identically
the same misfortune. There are few sadder contrasts than
those presented in the life of Galileo. His use of the
pendulum as a means of measuring time, his promulgation

GALILEO'S TOWER.

of the three laws of motion, his
wonderful invention of the telescope,
his adoption of the Copernican system of astronomy, and his
announcement to the world of the four satellites of Jupiter,
the solar spots, and the fact that the Milky Way, spanning the heavens with its arch of worlds, was in reality the
luminous pathway of innumerable suns, drew to him crowds
of pupils from all parts of Europe. But, alas! we recollect
that while these teachings crowned him with a deathless fame,
they temporarily made for him more foes than friends, till he
was finally forced to abjure as false some of his great discoveries. Whether or not we accept as true the legend that,
on rising from his recantation of the doctrine of our planet's
motion round the sun, he spoke the famous words, "*E pur
si muove!*" (It does move though!) we know it was his melancholy fate to die without beholding the triumph of those

truths, which he yet felt convinced must finally prevail, as they now do, forming the very rudiments of our children's education.

Every visitor to Florence walks or drives by an admirable carriage road to the height of San Miniato, which is surmounted by a famous church founded in honor of St. Minias, who suffered martyrdom on this hill in the third century of the Christian era. Near by is a sharp projection in a massive wall half overgrown with ivy. It is a part of the old rampart constructed, in 1529, by Michelangelo, who was not only sculptor, painter, architect, and poet, but also a civil engineer of the Republic, and superintended here for months the defense of Florence against a foreign foe. In memory of this greatest of all Florentines, a spacious square has been constructed on the hill, and in the centre stands a fine bronze copy of his David. Michelangelo was particularly fond of the view of Florence from this height, and I was told that, during her residence here, George Eliot, also, came frequently at sunset to gaze from San Miniato on the city of the Renaissance, and muse upon its glorious history.

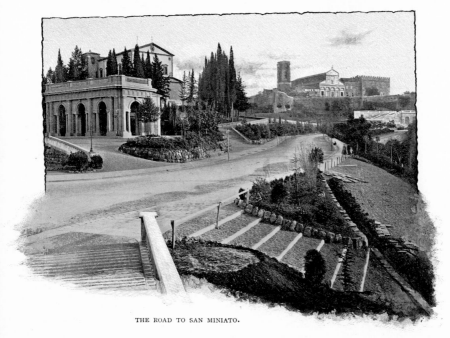

THE ROAD TO SAN MINIATO.

THE CEMETERY OF SAN MINIATO.

Upon the terraces near the church, above the City of the Living, lies a City of the Dead. I know of nothing in the world quite like this Florentine Campo Santo; for, elevated in the sight of all, it seems symbolical of an intermediate step, — a halting-place midway between earth and heaven. Here, in rectangular enclosures, exquisitely cared for, are many tombs; some of them stately marble structures, but most of them plain graves, each covered with a marble tombstone bearing an inscription. From these a cross or shaft occasionally rises, but no monotonous regularity is discernible. Broad paths wind in and out among these gardens of the dead, and, standing here and looking down upon the noble city filled with its inspiring memories, this cemetery seemed to me the spot above all others in the world where, if I were a Florentine, I should desire to rest.

In Italy the dead have festivals as well as the living, and on the first and second days of November this cemetery is the

THE INTERIOR OF SAN MINIATO.

favorite resort of Florentines. Beautiful floral decorations
are then lavished on the graves, many of which are buried
deep in mounds of flowers, while the large tombs resemble
temporary gardens, their marble walls being almost entirely
concealed by stately plants, garlands of trailing ferns and
grasses, and wreaths and crosses woven out of lovely blossoms.
On such occasions, the whole character of the cemetery seems
changed; for the white gravestones are then rich with color,
the rose leaf has replaced the cypress, and Death has abdi-
cated temporarily to Life.

Among the prominent mausoleums here is that of the
family of Tommaso Salvini, whose rank as the greatest tragedian of modern times can hardly be disputed. Though seventy
years of age, the illustrious actor is still hale and strong; but
he has now, save for an occasional charitable performance, left
the stage, to pass the evening of his life in calm retirement at
his Florentine villa, where he enjoys the memory of his artistic

SALVINI'S TOMB AT SAN MINIATO.

triumphs, especially those connected with his tours in America. It is in this tomb at San Miniato that the tragedian's body will finally repose, when it shall be no longer animated by his gifted spirit; but even now the sculptured sepulchre has for Americans a touching interest from the fact that the tragedian's son, Alessandro Salvini, is here buried. Many a visitor from the United States will halt before his resting-place above the City of Flowers; and remembering the genuine admiration he won, and his marriage to an American lady, many a rose they will lay tenderly upon the threshold of this house of death, freighted with grateful memories and sorrowful regrets that this young life of brilliant promise should have thus early ended in pathetic suffering.

TOMMASO SALVINI.

Standing beside his grave, as I recalled the characters in which he had afforded me such pleasure, I thought of the appropriate lines:

> " Two travel-worn and weary feet at rest
>   From paths of pain now shrouded in the past;
> Two cold hands crossed upon a pulseless breast
>   From which the soul has taken flight at last;
> Two eyes from whose dark vacant cells the glow
>   Of sunshine seems forever to have fled;
> Two mute lips, meeting like an unstrung bow,
>   From which the final arrow, speech, has sped!"

A view at sunset from this terrace, on a night in spring, forms one of my most treasured memories. A soft haze mellowed the historic city, and floated off beyond it to the purple hills. The sun hung on the verge of the horizon like a ball of molten gold. On its glowing disk the silhouette of the tower of the Palazzo Vecchio crept upward, little by little, until its apex

ALESSANDRO SALVINI.

pierced the upper solar rim, and the great yellow globe appeared to fall asunder and then vanish, as if the stony shaft had cleft it suddenly in twain and tossed it into the abyss of

SAN MINIATO, LOOKING TOWARD THE CITY.

night.   Later, a slender, crescent moon stole out upon the sky, so faint and fragile that it seemed more like the spirit than the body of the Queen of Heaven.   Still light enough remained to show the dome of Brunelleschi, like an inverted flower, or a silver bell, suspended from the star-gemmed dome of night of which it was the miniature replica.   Beside it rose the graceful shaft of Giotto's Campanile, — the wraith of a tower, rather than a monument of stone, — the upper part of which appeared to be detached from earth, and to be floating, spirit-like, in the mysteriously misty air.   It called to mind the Angel of the Annunciation, standing motionless, with folded arms and upward-pointed wings. Meantime, no sounds of the great city reached me ; and I could almost fancy that Florence was herself a mighty Campo Santo, and that her citizens had perished at the death of day.

NAPLES

NAPLES

THE Bay of Naples holds within its curving arms the history and the legends of two thousand years. Few spots on earth awaken such absorbing interest. Not one surpasses it in beauty. Even in this prosaic age it still remains a copious fountain of romance. Year after year, and century after century, the worshipers of Nature from all lands have come to render homage to its matchless shores, like the soft waves which steal in from the outer sea, kiss with a murmur of delight its crescent beach and then retire; but the fair bay remains the same, "a thing of beauty and a joy forever." Yet it is not merely Nature that attracts us to the Bay of Naples. Its placid surface is a magic mirror which to the thoughtful eye reflects the pageantry of ancient days, when the

THE BAY OF NAPLES.

world's commerce covered it with ships, and an imperial court adorned it with resplendent barges. Each graceful hill that rises from its waves, as well as every island that reposes, jewel-like, upon its gently undulating breast, is crowned with some distinguished memory. Each breeze that dimples its transparent surface whispers, to him who hears aright, the name of some illustrious Roman who once made this shore his home. Moreover, towering far above it to an elevation of four thou-

NEAR POSILIPO.

sand feet, rises that dark volcanic cone, Vesuvius, which even now holds up by day its smoking torch, and in the night seems threatening heaven with its shafts of fire; while to complete its mystery and charm, beside the changeless flood of this Vesuvian bay there lie two buried cities, slowly emerging from their lava shrouds after a sepulture of eighteen hundred years. These with a silent eloquence, incomparably more effective than all speech, are constantly reminding us not to forget amid the fleeting present the grandeur of a mighty past. Well was the city which arose here named by the ancients after Parthenope, a siren! For this enchanting region has entranced the hearts of all men from the time of Homer to our own. It has the form

NAPLES.

of a gigantic amphitheatre, of which the arena is the sea.
Vesuvius is in the centre, and on either side of it extends
a crescent fifteen miles in length.   This is, indeed, part of
the hallowed ground of ancient Italy.   Around it the mythology of Greece and Rome has cast a never-dying charm.   The
very air seems tremulous with classic memories.   At every
step we pass the site of some imperial palace or patrician villa.
Vineyards and gardens still adorn these slopes, as when they
furnished wine to Horace and to Hadrian; and on the hillside
of Posilipo, beneath which

> " swells and falls
> The bay's deep breast at intervals,"

once stood the homes of Cicero and Virgil.

Below the place where they resided the hill is perforated
by a tunnel through which Roman emperors have passed.   It
was in use when Christ was born, and during nineteen hundred
years its roof has
echoed to the
various languages
of those who, in
successive centu-
ries, were masters
of this shore.
Quite recently,
however, the roof
of this gloomy
vault, as if unable
longer to sup-
port the burden
of its memories,
fell in with a tre-
mendous crash,
and it is now a
ruin. A new one,

THE OLD TUNNEL.

close at hand, has
been opened to
replace it, but I
could not see in
it much improve-
ment over its
predecessor; for,
though a trifle
wider, a part of
it is the track of
a steam tram-
way. On more
than one occa-
sion the loco-
motive met our
carriage here,

THE NEW TUNNEL.

startling the horse, and seeming like some old dragon of
mythology rushing to seize its prey; since in this cavern,

only forty feet
in width, the
iron monster's
panting breath
and heavy tread
were by rever-
beration multi-
plied a hundred-
fold, till we
could almost
fancy that the
mountain, with
a savage roar,
was crashing
down to grind
us into powder.

VIEW FROM VIRGIL'S TOMB.

Emerging with relief from this dark tunnel, we climbed the cliff and stood upon the hill which will be ever memorable as the home of the poet Virgil. Here, with perhaps the loveliest view on earth outspread before him, he composed his two great works, the "Georgics" and "Æneid," whose glory has outlived by many centuries the Roman Empire itself. The word Posilipo means "freedom from sorrow" and, apparently, the poet found the situation worthy of its name; for when he died at Brindisi, just nineteen years before the birth of Christ, he begged the Emperor Augustus, with whom he was then traveling, to see that his remains were brought back and buried on this hill. This the Emperor, who greatly admired and

VIRGIL'S TOMB.

loved him, ordered to be done. Inspired by these memories I stooped and entered a small low-roofed structure, known as the Tomb of Virgil. Upon a marble slab erected there I read the brief and modest epitaph composed by Virgil himself, which may be translated freely thus:

> "In lovely Mantua was my childhood's home,
> Till my ambition lured me forth to Rome;
> Flocks, fields, and heroes have inspired my breast;
> And now on Naples' sunny slope I rest."

Below this, on the pedestal, are cut the words: "Conse-crated to the Prince of Latin poets by F. G. Eichhoff, Librarian to her Majesty, the Queen of France, 1840." This is only one of many attempts to honor Virgil's final resting-place; but, thus far, all such monuments have either fallen into decay, or have been carried away by relic hunters. Yet, since the historic site is undoubtedly genuine, thousands of grateful pilgrims come here year after year, and the poet's genius still exists, as fade-

ON THE NORTH SHORE.

less and immortal as the beauty of the bay. Standing by Virgil's tomb, and looking off on the adjacent shore where St. Paul landed when he came to Italy, I thought of the not improbable legend that he then paid a visit to the poet's grave. This was in fact commemorated by a verse, frequently sung in Roman Catholic churches during the Middle Ages, which ran as follows:

"When to Virgil's tomb they brought him,
Tender grief and pity wrought him
To exclaim with pious tears:
'What a saint I might have crowned thee,
Had I only, living, found thee,
Poet, first and without peers.'"

Continuing our drive beyond Posilipo, along the northern shore, we soon approached the modern town of Pozzuoli. It

POSILIPO.

is the unseen that most interests us here; for this, in ancient times, was a seaport of so much importance that Cicero called it a "miniature Rome." When, in the dawn of the Christian era, St. Paul set foot upon this shore, he doubtless saw around him a multitude of ware-

THE COAST NEAR POZZUOLI.

houses, and stately ships unloading oil from Athens, corn from Egypt, grain from Sicily, African lions destined for Italian amphi-

THE AMPHITHEATRE AT POZZUOLI.

theatres, and spoils from every portion of the Roman world. Before him then upon these hills rose, tier on tier, hundreds of marble villas, temples, and magnificent baths and, above all, the walls of a huge amphitheatre, in which no less than thirty thousand people could be seated.

NEAPOLITAN FISHERMEN.

Now all this splendor has departed. The hollow-eyed inhabitants look like beggars in a ruined banquet-hall. Gone are the villas, palaces, and baths of Puteoli, as it was then called, and the once crowded waters of its famous harbor are now rarely furrowed by a keel. One ruin here impressed me greatly. Emerging from the bay, not far from the land, are thirteen columns which formerly supported the great landing-pier of the city. So massive is the lava concrete which encases them, that, notwithstanding all the ravages of war, and waves, and earthquake shocks for eighteen hundred years, it still remains as strong as when upon the platform it upheld the great Apostle landed on his way to Rome.

There is, however, a present as well as a past to Pozzuoli, of which we are convinced by the appearance of its fishermen along the beach. Although they look almost as ancient as the ruins that surround

LANDING THE NETS.

them, they are not really old. Their wrinkles come from
hard work and exposure. This Neapolitan bay, which is
to us merely a thing of beauty, is to these men a vast
arena where they struggle for existence. The stake is life
itself, their foe starvation. Even if they, to-day, come off
victorious, they gain as their reward merely a respite from
the conflict for twenty-four hours; then the grim fight begins
again. Life on the Neapolitan shore is not entirely composed
of merriment. The singers and guitarists, whose music echoes
softly over the bay, are never genuine fishermen. The actual
toilers of the sea have little time to sing. Day after day, year
after year, beneath a scorching sun, or face to face with wintry
winds, they work for what amounts at best to only a bare sub-
sistence. For, though the bay is deep and wide, and life abundant in its waves, many are the boatmen who cast in their nets.
The very best wages they can earn do not exceed a dollar a day.

Driving on from Pozzuoli, another indentation of the coast
revealed to us the little island, Nisida, — only a tiny spot of
earth, but rich with memories that held us spellbound. To
a villa on this wave-encircled
rock, Brutus retired after the

NISIDA.

murder of Cæsar, and hither Cicero came to hold with him
a consultation. A crisis had indeed arrived accentuated by
Mark Antony's great speech. The cruel murder in the Senate-
House was meeting with no popular approval. Brutus and
Cassius, with their followers, had struck down the first man
of the world, but the conditions that had made him necessary
were beyond their reach. "We have killed the King," cried
Cicero, sadly,
"but the kingdom
is still with us."

BAIÆ.

Here, also,
after their inter-
view, Cicero and
Brutus parted
from each other
never to meet
again : one to re-
turn to Rome, to
perish by the
emissaries of
Mark Antony;
the other to join
Cassius at Phi-
lippi, and there to
fall upon his own sword after defeat upon the field of battle.
It was on this island, too, that Brutus, with a premonition of
approaching death, spoke the farewell to his wife, Portia,
which Shakespeare has immortalized; and here, on learning
of her husband's death, Portia committed suicide. Such are
a few of the impressive memories of Nisida; and yet, to-day,
it still floats smilingly upon the sparkling bay, unconscious
now, as then, of all the scenes of human suffering of which
it has been frequently the stage.
  Not far from Nisida, we reached the limit of our northern

THE QUAY OF SANTA LUCIA.

drive, — the ruined town of Baiæ. When one beholds the few
poor fragments standing here, it is difficult to imagine how this
must have looked nineteen hundred years ago. Then its enchanting beach was fringed with palaces. It was the most
magnificent watering-place in the whole Roman world, and
filled with admiration and surprise even visitors from Rome.
All the great poets of that time speak of its luxury as something marvelous.
"No bay in the
world," writes
Horace, "sur-
passes that
of beautiful
Baiæ." Cæ-
sar, Pompey,
Caligula, Ne-
ro, Hadrian,
and many
other famous
Romans of
antiquity had
villas here;
and where
the emper-

RUINS AT BAIÆ.

ors led the nobles followed fast. The wealthy families of Rome
so crowded to this place, that the long Appian way approaching
it was, in the season, thronged with chariots and gilded litters,
and every nook of land was taken for their dwellings. In fact,
so gorgeous were these seaside villas, that Baiæ's crescent beach
was called the Golden Shore; but since those days both man
and nature seem to have combined to make the place a scene of
desolation. Repeated earthquake shocks, the sinking of the
harbor's edge below the level of the sea, and the destruction
wrought by Goths and Saracens have thoroughly effaced all

THE SQUARE AND CASTLE OF ST. ELMO, NAPLES.

proofs of Baiæ's luxury, save such as I beheld in the clear sunlight, when, leaning over the gunwale of the boat, I caught a glimpse of blocks of marble and mosaic pavements lying far below like prisoners in an ocean cave.

The environs of Naples form a Paradise, but Naples itself is, to put it mildly, a Purgatory. It is true that great improvements have been made here in the last few years. Many old and filthy alleys have been transformed into spacious thoroughfares. Upon the heights, especially, new streets, apartment houses, and hotels have been constructed, which lift the tourist far above the pandemonium below, and let him (while his other senses rest) feast his

THE NEW GALLERY, NAPLES.

eyes only on the grand, incomparable view. In the heart
of the city, also, there is one admirable structure of recent
origin. It is a high-roofed, finely decorated promenade, the
cost of which was about four million dollars. In some respects
it is superior to the Gallery of Victor Emmanuel in Milan, which
it resembles, and has the form of a gigantic cross with arms of
well-nigh equal length. Roofed in with glass, its crystal dome
rises two hundred feet above the marble pavement. Along its

NARROW STREETS.

sides are cafés and attractive shops and, in the evening, music
gives this brilliant passageway an added charm. Still, these
new Neapolitan features do not wholly change the old and most
conspicuous characteristics of the city, — noise, rags, dirt, and
donkeys.

One appreciates this fact, especially, when standing on the
famous quay of Santa Lucia and looking at two or three of the
streets, if such they can be called, which here pour forth their

A STREET GROUP.

torrents of humanity, as muddy streams discharge their contents into the sea. Some of these alleys are but six feet wide, and seem even narrower by reason of the gloomy tenements which rise on either side to an amazing height, and only stop where poverty itself will climb no higher. The windows in these swarming hives are always filled with unkempt heads. From one brink to the other, unwashed hands can almost meet across the dismal chasm. Ropes zigzag back and forth like trolley wires, and serve as clotheslines for the luckless beings who wait there, restless as caged animals, until their solitary indispensables are dry enough to wear again. Men, women, goats, cows, donkeys, and a host of children swarm here like flies around a sugar cask. During the day they live in the noisy streets, and at night most of them are huddled into little rooms, some of which have no windows and

HAIR-DRESSING.

A NAPLES STREET.

no chimneys. Within these fetid cells, and often on one enormous bed, repose sometimes a dozen human beings of all ages and both sexes. The only heat they ever get is from a portable charcoal stove, which is frequently taken into the street for cooking purposes. Among these people women, as well as men, perform a great deal of their dressing and undressing in the open thoroughfares, with absolute indifference to the passer-by. The women's hair is usually in wild disorder; but on Sunday or a festival day these Neapolitan females carefully arrange their thick, black tresses, and with a touching spirit of self-sacrifice spend hours in combing one another's heads. On such occasions nothing could induce me to pass through one of the narrow streets. The toilet-making of the children is much simpler. It does not differ much from that of a dog. Both have the same acute but fleeting trials, which must be overcome in much the same way. In viewing them, I could not doubt the truth of the proverb that it is the little things in life that most annoy us.

NEAPOLITAN BOY.

Moreover, the garments of a Neapolitan boy are fully open to the breezes from the bay; and as these constitute his only clothes, he wears them till they drop to pieces or else are, patch by patch, so thoroughly renewed that — like the famous knife which had in turn new blades and a new handle, yet was still the same — he finally acquires on the same old model a new set of rags.

You can imagine, then, that amid such surroundings a walk or drive through Naples presents some startling surprises. On leaving my hotel one morning, the first thing I encountered was a flock of goats which, though belonging to the gentler sex, marched along as proudly as a Prussian regiment in Berlin. At frequent intervals these little wandering dairies halted, while one of them, obedient to her driver's call, climbed the stairs of an apartment house from which a signal had been given. If milk was wanted on the ground floor, some member of the family brought out a pail, or even a bottle, to be filled.

AN ITINERANT DAIRY.

At other times, I saw these articles lowered in a basket from an upper story, to be drawn up again by strings. Cows are, also, driven through many of the Neapolitan streets and, like the goats, are milked upon the sidewalks, at so much a pint. I have often had to step aside for them while thus engaged. Whatever, therefore, may be said about the unwholesome meats and vegetables in their markets, the Neapolitans beyond a doubt secure fresh milk. The owners of the cows and

COOKING OMELETS.

goats, however, seemed profoundly sad. They are the only men in Italy who cannot cheat. I did not dare inform them of the privileges of our milkmen. If I had told them that in free America the milk is frequently diluted, and that the cans are sometimes rinsed with impure water, conveying thus to hundreds of consumers germs of typhoid fever, they might at once have emigrated to the United States. Another characteristic scene in Neapolitan streets is a portable kitchen and lunch-counter where fish, fruit, cakes, and various kinds of soup are sold in portions costing about a cent. They are the cafés of the *lazzaroni*, the homeless vagabonds of Naples who live without working, and who, if they should ever so far forget themselves as to do a stroke of honest labor, would no longer be *lazzaroni*. For most of these people meat, even of the poorest kind, is an unlooked-for luxury. Even macaroni, on which we generally suppose the Neapolitans exist, is too expensive for the poorest classes, save upon rare occasions,

A MIDDAY LUNCH.

when, almost breathless with delight, they eat it with tomatoes, and in their subsequent dreams are quite unable to distinguish heaven from spaghetti. When a tourist has watched the manufacture of macaroni in Naples — has seen the filthy men who make it and, finally, beholds great sheets of it hung up to dry like portières of yellow beads, amidst the dust, rags, and wretchedness of Neapolitan streets — he gives a new interpretation to the ancient proverb, "See Naples and die." My

DRYING MACARONI.

friend was almost ill from merely recollecting that he had eaten macaroni here the night before, and nothing would induce him after that to touch the dish, however skillfully prepared; but to a Neapolitan *lazzaroni* such squeamishness appears incredible.

One night, in driving through a market-place, we saw a vender of spaghetti. Stopping the carriage, I paid him to distribute twenty platefuls to the people, that we might watch

MACARONI EATERS.

them eat it. The rumor of this spread like wildfire, and in three minutes our cab was like an island in a sea of roaring, struggling humanity. In vain the vender tried to single out one person at a time. The instant that one wretched man received a plate a dozen others jumped for it; and four or five black fists grabbed handfuls of the steaming mass, and thrust the almost scalding mixture down their throats. I had expected to be amused, but this mad eagerness for common food denoted actual hunger. Some famished-looking women and children seemed so disappointed at not getting any that my heart ached for them. The poverty

"BREATHLESS WITH DELIGHT."

THREE OF A KIND.

of Naples is distressing, and to most of these poor vagabonds life is a desperate struggle for existence. Some years ago the Italian Senator, Professor Villari, investigated the condition of the poor of Naples, and his report reveals a depth of misery which, without such authority, would seem incredible. It is estimated that there are in Naples hundreds of children who have practically never known father or mother, and who live for the most part on the refuse of the streets, and sleep on church steps or in empty boxes. Others perhaps, less fortunate, are huddled into horrible window-less tenements, which a German doctor calls "the most ghastly human dwellings on the face of the earth." At least a quarter of a million human beings in Naples literally live from hand to mouth. Thousands of them have no home whatever. They sleep in kennels and dark corners, they rob the dying of their clothes, and are perpetually hungry. I was informed that, on an average, four or five people die here daily of starvation. Physicians call it heart-failure or exhaustion, but the cause is really lack of food.

Every great metropolis has, of course, a large amount of poverty and suffering, but I believe that in no other European city are these evils so frightfully evident, when one looks a little below the surface, as in Naples. The official report of the Royal Commissary to King Humbert, in 1892, says. "For six months a famished mob has thronged the staircase of the municipality. In this multitude are children of both sexes absolutely destitute, mothers with dying babies at their milk-less breasts, and widows followed by a tribe of almost naked children, together with the aged and infirm, all hungry and in rags. One can," he adds, "but marvel at the docile nature of the Neapolitans who bear with resignation such unutterable misery." It must not be supposed, however, that efforts are not made to help these sufferers. In 1885 the King issued an order for the better housing of the poor in Naples, and a gift of ten million dollars and a loan of an equal sum were made for the same object. Much has been done in giving the city better drain-age and a good supply of healthful drinking water; but other improvements have been slow, fettered by red tape, hindered by much dishonesty, and, worst of all, blindly opposed in many cases by the superstitious and ignorant people themselves.

In a recent visit to Naples the lower classes seemed to me more destitute and wretched than they had been a score of years before. The principal cause for this increase of misery

FAINT FROM EXHAUSTION.

is, I believe, the present military system of the Government. To maintain this, to build enormous battleships, and to keep up expensive African colonies, the people have been literally taxed to death.   Italian ministers must rack their brains to invent new taxes.   There is, for example, a tax on every box of matches that some poor woman tries to sell for a cent, a tax on every one who offers in the street a bit of fruit or fish, and a tax on every name displayed outside a building.   The latest invention of the Italian minister of finance is a tax on empty bottles. I threw away one at Sorrento.   A native told me that he wanted it, but that if he picked it up and brought it into Naples he would have to pay for the privilege.   The wandering street musicians, also, have to pay a tax; so do the news-boys, guides, tram-car drivers, waiters in restaurants, and even the beggars who must have a license to solicit alms. Each village has its local cus-tom-house. In driving the few miles from Naples to Sorrento we passed half a dozen of them; and every particle of food or merchandise which the half-starved inmates of those small towns brought in for their use was subject to a duty.   Grapes are taxed on the vines when about half ripe.   If, after that, they spoil, so much the worse for their owners; for the Government pays no money back. Moreover, wholesome, nourishing food is beyond the reach of the poor.   Beef, for example, costs in Naples thirty cents a

NAPLES GAMINS.

EARNING TEN CENTS A DAY PLAITING STRAW.

pound, and butter forty cents; good milk sells at twelve cents a quart, and goat's milk at fourteen cents; while a small chicken, which will not however tear under the wing, commands a price of sixty cents. Kerosene, also, costs nearly four times as much in Naples as in America; fuel is so dear that, among the very poor, vegetables are not boiled, but merely softened in hot water to save the long-continued use of the fire; and it is a pitiable sight to see old women or children buying a handful of charcoal at a time to do the cooking for the day. Yet, on account of the prevailing dishonesty in Italy, it is said that not more than two-thirds of the revenue from these taxes ever reaches the public treasury.

It is, in my opinion, a terrible mistake for Italy to try to keep in step with Germany, France,

A STREET SCENE, NAPLES.

CRISPI.

and England. She has been flattered and cajoled into assuming a position in the politics of Europe which she cannot fill. She is doing what in an individual would be called "living beyond his means." It would be vastly better for her were she content to rank with Belgium, Switzerland, and Holland as a minor power. Her soil is supremely fertile; she is the chief custodian of ancient Art, the favorite of Nature, and the shrine of History. She should also be preëminently the land of Peace. The multitude of tourists and pilgrims — who every year enter her gates and spend their money freely in her cities — would make her prosperous were not one-half of her revenues used to pay the national debt, and if two-thirds of the remaining half were not expended on an army and a navy suitable only to a first-class, wealthy nation.

Some landowners in Italy claim that they pay nearly sixty per cent. of their income in taxes to the Government. An American who owns property in Italy states that he pays on the assessed income from a few acres of land forty-two per cent.; on the assessed rent of his house over twenty-three per cent.; and

INTERIOR OF THE ROYAL PALACE, NAPLES.

NAPLES LIFE.

there is no limit of estate, real or personal, below which taxation is not applied. One bad result of this excessive burden is the enormous emigration from Italy; and another, equally disastrous to the welfare of the country, is the immense area of farm land which is confiscated by the Government for unpaid taxes, and can neither be sold nor cultivated.

In viewing the splendor of the Royal Palace in Naples, which presents such a striking contrast to the misery of the people, one naturally asks, "Is the King popular with his subjects?" Undoubtedly. If things go wrong, the blame is laid not upon him, but on his ministers; and, while he is admired everywhere in Italy, in Naples he is adored. The Neapolitans, poor and wretched though they are, know that the King at least is thoroughly devoted to their welfare. They can never forget his conduct at the outbreak of the cholera in 1884. He was in his

NEAPOLITAN MISERY.

bed, at Rome, ill with fever, when he was awakened at midnight by a dispatch informing him that cholera had begun to rage with violence in Naples. He rose at once, despite the protests of his doctor, ordered a special train and in two hours was on his way to the plague-stricken city. He had expected to go next day to Monza, where a magnificent reception was awaiting him; but he telegraphed to the authorities there: "Banquet at Monza; cholera at Naples; I am going to Naples. If you don't see me again,

KING HUMBERT.

good-by." "When I read a copy of that telegram," said a Neapolitan to me, "I shed tears like a child; and I pray God, if any anarchist ever throws dynamite at my King, that I may be there to receive the blow and give my life for him."

On reaching Naples, King Humbert found only the common people at the station to receive him. The rich, the aristocracy, and even most of the officials had fled. The King, however, did not care for that. It was the people he had come to save. For weeks he worked incessantly to check the plague and to relieve the sufferers; he entered the hospitals, took the hands of the sick and dying in his own, and by his example shamed others into duty. After a week, one of his ministers said to him: "Your Majesty, there were three thousand, four hundred cases yesterday. This is getting to be alarming. Ought you not to return to Rome?" "You may go if you like," replied the King, "I shall remain till I see Naples free from cholera." And he kept his word.

Fortunately, the tourist does not always see the mournful side of Naples. Wandering minstrels, for example, greet him everywhere. Our ocean steamer had not come

SANTA LUCIA.

THE RIVIERA.

to anchor in the bay, before some boatloads of musicians were around us, making the air resound with the familiar songs of "Santa Lucia," and "Faniculi-Fanicula." A new relay awaited us beneath the hotel balcony; and on the boats to Capri and Sorrento, accordeons, violins, and mandolins were kept busily at work; while now and then a plaintive voice sang an air from "Trovatore," or murmured in pathetic tones, *"Addio, bella Napoli."* Nor was this all; for, after the singing, words and music were offered for sale by the musicians with a proud confidence that this could never do them harm; much as a "lightning calculator" sells his books, to show how to accomplish what in reality he alone can do.

Another interesting feature of popular life in Naples is the story-teller. I do not now refer to liars. I fear that such a category would include pretty nearly the entire population. I mean the man who reads

WANDERING MINSTRELS.

or recites for the amusement of the crowd; and even in Naples there are those who deem themselves sufficiently rich to pay half a cent to be thus entertained. Whenever the story-teller is a man of ability, the scene is sure to be dramatic, because every Italian is a natural actor. His gestures form a language in themselves. No sentence seems complete without them; and when excited a Neapolitan, especially, gesticulates so fast that he appears to be boxing with an unseen foe.

THE STORY-TELLER.

Still another characteristic sight in Neapolitan streets is the public letter-writer. I saw these scriveners everywhere a score of years ago, and even recently I found them yet employed in certain quarters of the city, especially on Sunday afternoons; for, notwithstanding the popular education which prevails in Italy, the public letter-writer's occupation is not gone. In 1863 ninety per cent. of the Neapolitan population could neither read nor write! Then these professional scribes were almost a necessity. Under the present Government immense improvement has been made; but when we reflect how great is the effort for an illiterate person to express his thoughts on paper, it is not strange that the old fashion still prevails. When I could do so, unobserved, I watched this business with much interest. There is so much to study in the different applicants! Their faces always tell the story. A man, for example, will appear awkward, bashful and laughing foolishly

at any term of endearment that he whispers to the scribe; and
he may be succeeded by a pretty girl, whose flashing eyes and
trembling lips betray her jealous doubts and anger at not hearing from her absent lover; while another characteristic person
here is an aged mother who murmurs in a feeble voice some
tender message for her absent boy, a conscript in the army. In
contrast to all this, the scribe himself is almost as machine-like
as the pen he wields. The stories are old to him. Accordingly
he writes, cold and impassive as a telegraph wire, which, with
complete indifference, transmits the news of life or death along
its metal thread.

When in the company of Italians, particularly in Naples,
I have often noticed in all classes indications of the singular
superstition known as *jettatura*, or the "evil eye." Educated
and cultivated people, it is true, affect to laugh at it, as foreigners do, and call it childish folly; but
many of them are quite as
ready to make, in secret, the
sign which they believe

THE LETTER-WRITER.

averts the evil spell, as some Americans are to see the new moon over the right shoulder, or to avoid commencing a journey on Friday. It is quite generally believed by Italians that certain people can bring misfortune, either purposely or unintentionally, by the glance of the eye, and that the only antidote for such a calamity, when in the presence of such persons, is to hold the forefinger and little finger pointed outward, while the rest of the hand is closed. The wearing of coral is also

THE CARRICELLO.

thought to be of great use in averting the effects of *jettatura*, particularly if it be in the form of a little charm, shaped like two horns. Just what excites the suspicion that an individual has the "evil eye," I have never been able to ascertain, but, probably, it is the result of some unfortunate coincidence, or, possibly, of ill-will on the part of the first accuser. Happily, the supposed possessor of the fatal gift is frequently entirely unconscious of the power attributed to him; for, as a rule, however much his presence may be dreaded, he will not see any outward manifestation of that feeling. The initiated observer, however, will perhaps detect in several members of the company a hasty gesture of the hand behind the back or under the table. To point the fingers openly toward any one would be an unpardonable insult. That this superstition and its antidote are of great antiquity, and have been legitimately inherited by

THE TARANTELLA.

the modern Italians, is proved by the interesting fact that some of the bodies excavated in Pompeii have the hands closed and the two fingers extended in the identical gesture frequently made use of at the present time.

Mount Vesuvius is to the Neapolitan bay what Fujiyama is to many a landscape of Japan, — the lofty background of the picture, and the grand presiding genius of the place. By day it proudly waves its plume of smoke, by night its torch of fire, as if it claimed to be the champion of destruction. It has two parts: one standing as firm as the eternal hills, the other varying with

ROAD TO VESUVIUS.

each new eruption. The former is the main body of the mountain; the latter is its cone, up to the base of which an admirable carriage road has been constructed.

The modern Vesuvius has not the appearance that it presented two thousand years ago. When Cæsar looked upon it from Baiæ, or Virgil from Posilipo, or when St. Paul beheld it, nineteen years before it overwhelmed Pompeii, it was not the gigantic lighthouse that it is to-day. It was a beautiful

LAVA AND CONE.

mountain then, clothed to the top with fertile fields and vineyards. Even its summit was a grassy plain, nine miles in circuit, and there the gladiator Spartacus and his companions kept for a time at bay an army sent out from Imperial Rome. Vesuvius, as it now appears, reveals a scene of frightful desolation. Over its sides has rolled repeatedly a perfect deluge of destruction, withering, burning, suffocating everything: first, with its scorching breath; then, with its thick, resistless tide of red-hot lava. This lava is now cold and petrified, resembling in some respects an Alpine glacier; only, instead of glittering ice, these billows are of inky blackness. It is, moreover, of enormous thickness. Unnumbered layers of it have been spread out here, until the mountain is a kind of palimpsest, on which the demon of destruction has, more than a score of times

THE ERUPTION OF 1872.

within the present century, written the records of its devastation
in characters of fire.   The eruption of 1872 was one of the
most tremendous since the destruction of Pompeii.   Filled to
the brim with molten lava, the mountain's fiery bowl was then
shattered by a fierce convulsion, and poured forth twenty million
cubic yards of liquid fire over a country filled with flowers and
blossoms.   One of the lava streams was three thousand feet
wide, twenty feet deep, and had a temperature   of two
thousand degrees, Fah-
renheit!

In the observatory
of Vesuvius, situated on

THE OBSERVATORY.

a spur of the mountain,
scientific men are stationed
to observe a delicate instrument which indicates by the vibrations
of a needle the degree of the volcano's activity.   It is, however,
a position of great danger.   In 1872 an awful wave of lava came
rolling toward this ledge as if to overwhelm it.   Happily, it
divided at the base of the cliff and went on either side; but,

when the divisions met again at its lower extremity the director, Palmieri, and his comrades found themselves encircled by a sea of fire. In 1875 I saw and talked with Palmieri, and it was thrilling to hear him describe the heat which then for days was so intense as well-

LAVA.

nigh to destroy them, the red-hot stones which fell around them from a fearful height, and the extraordinary grandeur of the flood of fire.

"Would you remain through another such eruption?" I asked him.

"Certainly," he replied, "my life belongs to science. If the observatory falls, I wish to fall with it."

Advancing beyond this point to the base of the cone, I found that an amazing change had taken

THE RAILWAY.

place here since my previous visits. Where I had formerly
climbed fifteen hundred feet through lava ashes ankle-deep, an
open car, on a wire-rope railway, now transports the tourist almost
to the crater. This method of conveyance looks extremely peril-
ous ; but, in reality, beneath the shifting ashes is a bed of lava,
as hard as granite ; and unless torn to pieces by some great eruption, I see no reason why this railroad, resting upon such a foun-

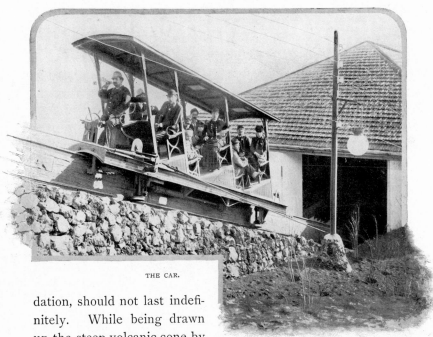

THE CAR.

dation, should not last indefinitely. While being drawn
up the steep volcanic cone by
steam power, as easily as up the Rigi, I thoroughly appreciated
the difference between this mode of travel and the terribly fa-
tiguing climb of former times. As the cone has an inclination
of from forty-five to sixty-three degrees, it is almost impossible to
gain a genuine foothold. In the old way of making the ascent I
would slip back at every step almost as far as I advanced, and
every few minutes had to halt for breath. I find, in looking over
my old note-books, both times that I climbed the cone I was an

ON THE SHOULDERS.

hour in reaching the summit; but that, on the other hand, I came down again in four and a half minutes, descending at a break-neck speed, when once started in the slippery, sliding ashes. Even by the new mode of ascending Vesuvius, when we arrived at the upper terminus of the cable road, we found that we could still enjoy a little sample of the old style of mountain climbing; for, of course, the railroad does not go actually to the crater. That would be foolhardy, since this fiery workshop of Vulcan is by no means tranquil. About two hundred and fifty feet of the mountain, there-

IN THE CHAIR.

fore, must be vanquished in the ancient fashion. A score of guides rushed forward to assist us, and offered for our aid and comfort a most embarrassing variety of canes, straps, and chairs, in addition to their own shoulders. We did not hesitate. The sun was hot, the ashes uninviting. Moreover, as Napoleon once said in reference to dancing, "forty years are forty years." I therefore took a chair which three unhappy men solemnly swore they would not drop, while my comrade got astride the shoulders of a stalwart guide. Thus mounted we exclaimed, "Excelsior!"

In fifteen minutes we had reached the edge of the crater. Below us was a monstrous cauldron, half a mile in width and hundreds of feet deep. When the white smoke allowed us

LOOKING INTO THE CRATER.

to observe the sides of the abyss, we saw that they were colored yellow, red, and purple, like the walls of the Grand Cañon of the Yellowstone. The ground around the crater was so hot that the soles of our boots were scorched, and a stick thrust an inch or two below the surface burst into a flame. Clouds of sulphurous smoke rolled up from the great void, continually. At intervals of two or three minutes, a dull explosion was heard below, a sheet of flame flashed before us like a fiery curtain, and red-hot stones were hurled to a height of seventy feet above our heads. These usually fell back into the crater; but twice they came beyond the edge, and struck the cone so near to us that we beat a hasty retreat. I thought then, and I still think, that when the mountain is as active as it was that summer, no matter what the guides may say, there is a risk in going to the crater; and when at night, from our hotel in Naples, we watched the showers of rocks shoot up like red-hot shells into the vault of night, we shuddered as we remembered

RAILWAY AND VALLEY.

how near we had stood to them a few hours before.

Only two weeks after our departure from Naples Vesuvius showed again its fearful power of destruction. Once more a gaping wound burst open in the monster's side, and from it molten lava poured forth in a fiery flood. The very carriage road over which we had driven fifteen days before was covered with a lurid stream three hundred feet in breadth. As, day by day, in northern Europe we read accounts of this eruption, how deeply we regretted that it had not taken place a fortnight earlier. But as it was, we saw enough to appreciate the words of Goethe, when he compared Vesuvius to a peak of hell rising out of Paradise.

From the volcano we naturally made our way to the most

A POMPEIAN STREET.

interesting of its victims, — Pompeii. I shall always remember the moment, when, having left our carriage outside in the dusty thoroughfare I stood, for the first time, before the ancient entrance to the buried town. I felt as if I were assisting at a miracle; for I was standing on the threshold of a resurrected city, and was about to see the incarnation of antiquity. Spectres of human beings have, it is said, appeared at various times and places in this world, but only here can one behold the ghost of a metropolis. The world has only one Pompeii.

We passed on through the ancient gate, which formerly was the principal exit to the sea, and found ourselves in one of the Pompeian streets. The

THE MARINE GATE.

first impression made upon me by this city was that of amazement at its preservation. Eighteen hundred years since it was filled with joyous life? Impossible! At the first glance one might conclude it had been ruined only half a century ago.

FORUM AND ARCH.

Pompeii has risen from the grave and cast aside part of her ashen burial robe, and, although dead, is still almost as well preserved as when she was entombed. Instinctively I looked around me here for people, but neither in the buildings nor in the streets appeared a single living being. I listened, but these desolate pavements gave echo to no footsteps save our own.

The second impression made upon me by Pompeii was that of silence. Its stillness haunted me. Behind us was the brilliant shore swarming with life, and almost deafening in its up-

STEPPING-STONES.

roar; but all these miles of empty streets were speechless and the houses tenantless. Under a burning sun there was no dust; within the ruts there rolled no chariot wheels. In the gay colonnades and courts to right and left we heard no music and no laughter; yet, after all, we would not have it otherwise. The genius of Pompeii is Solitude, — the natural guardian of all ruins, without which we could never feel the fascination of their history. Meantime, the original buildings were around us everywhere. It is true only their lower stories remain, for the upper portions, chiefly made of wood, were set on fire and consumed by live ashes from Vesuvius; and yet this is the same pavement on which the old Pompeians passed when Jesus walked in

A POMPEIAN HOUSE.

Galilee; and here, raised to a level with the curb, are the ancient stepping-stones, pressed often, doubtless, by the sandaled feet of fair Pompeian ladies. Between them, also, are the marks made by the wheels of vehicles, and cut perhaps more deeply on the fatal night when all were fleeing for their lives.

The dwellings of Pompeii were built in semi-Oriental style, and would, apparently, indicate that the climate of southern Italy was warmer then than now. Certainly one of the present Italian winters in these homes would be trying. A little distance from the door, the modern visitor invariably finds in every house a spacious court, surrounded on all sides by porticos. Unless an awning covered it, at least a portion of this court was always open to the sky, and in the centre was a marble basin, known as the *impluvium*, or receptacle for rain. In this, as in the Moorish courts of the Alhambra, a sweet-voiced fountain murmured day and night during the summer heat, lulling the inmates to repose. Beautiful flowers, also, frequently enclosed it, and from this perfumed courtyard the adjoining rooms

received their light and air. What most surprised me was the wonderful preservation of the frescos. Although the finest have been removed to the Museum at Naples, those which remain are often exquisite in form and color; and, when first unearthed, they frequently appear entirely undimmed

COURT AND IMPLUVIUM.

by their long burial of eighteen centuries. If a suitable roof were placed above them, they might last indefinitely; but Italy, alas, is spending too much money now on ironclads to lavish much upon Pompeii.

Every excavated dwelling here has an individuality peculiar to itself. Thus, one was recognized as a physician's house, because of surgical instruments discovered there; another, was identified by the address of a letter found in its courtyard and

deciphered; and
many have been
named from the
bronze seals be-
longing to their
owners. Among
the objects taken
from these
houses and now
preserved in the
Museum are
scales for weigh-
ing merchan-
dise; dishes for
cooking food;
carpenters'

FOUNTAIN AND FRESCOS.

planes and hammers; and, since the art of printing was then
unknown, contracts and deeds engraved either on bronze or

WEIGHTS AND MEASURES.

brass. Here, too,
are dentists' for-
ceps; instru-
ments of surgery,
resembling those
now in use; cos-
metics also,
rouge, curling
tongs, and
countless speci-
mens of jewelry,
—medallions,
gold pins, brace-
lets, and mag-
nificent cameos.
It is plain, then,

A MONEY CHEST.

that every-day life has not so greatly changed in eighteen hundred years; for, in these old Pompeian homes, we even saw hot-air flues for heating baths, and water pipes of lead with just such joints in them as plumbers make to-day.

Another interesting relic is a money chest, made of thick bronze, with decorations still intact and beautiful. From its great size it may be supposed that its owner was a banker. At all events, this miniature safe-deposit vault was much too large and ponderous to be carried off by robbers; yet I observed that the locks were not particularly strong. Probably servants watched it night and day, and on the threshold of the house in which it was discovered was

A POMPEIAN HOUSE RESTORED.

the mosaic of a ferocious monster, with the inscription, *"Cave Canem."*

How beautiful these dwellings must have been, with court-yards separated from one another by graceful columns bright with varied colors, most prominent of which was "Pompeian red"! The walls, also, were peopled with fair forms in fresco, and marble statues of the gods gleamed white against a crimson background; from frescoed ceilings, too, hung the exquisite bronze lamps, hundreds of which have been found; and gilded couches were in part concealed by draperies from Tyre or Damascus; while the pavements, many of which are still uninjured, were always of mosaic.

FRESCOS.

It is difficult to imagine anything more beautiful and durable in mural decorations than those which embellished the walls of these houses. If their apartments had been lined, like ours, with perishable paper, or if the paintings which adorned them had been hung from wooden cornices by picture hooks, we should now know, by observation, little about the interiors of Pompeian residences. But all these walls were made of stucco, hard and smooth as marble, and were not only tastefully colored, but bore upon their tinted surfaces charming frescos, that have outlasted eighteen centuries of burial. In Pompeii every house, and almost every room, was decorated with frescos illustrating Greek mythology, in which by means of graceful lines and rich, harmonious coloring, gods, goddesses, bacchantes, fauns, and centaurs were multiplied in infinite variety. Hundreds of landscape paintings, also, have been found on these walls, portraying, as a rule, the scenery of the coast about the Bay of Naples and the villas there.

SOLDIERS.

In their inspection of Pompeii, visitors are usually accompanied by one or more soldiers; since, were they absent, nothing would be safe. Relic-hunting is a mania everywhere; but in this resurrected city the temptation to pilfer or destroy seems to be overpowering. It is a sad fact that throughout the world the finest works of human genius and the most sacred memorials of history are not spared by man. Let but an earthquake or the lightning's bolt give one of them a blow, and there will speedily arrive vandals to desecrate the injured form, and, finally, relic-hunters like vultures to pick its bones. Why is it that we have Pompeii to-day? Because for centuries Vesuvius hid it from the sight of man.

In a wineshop we saw the frames for the *amphoræ*, or jars, all of which bore the marks of the name and quality of the liquor, as well as the year of its vintage, and which were found exactly where they had been placed by hands which have been dust for nearly two thousand years. Upon the counter, also, is a circular stain, left by the cup of one who may have quaffed here his last draught of wine made from the luscious grapes that grew on Mount Vesuvius. Close by this shop is a bakery, in the brick oven of which were found some carbonized loaves of bread that, no doubt, had been prepared for sale the evening of the city's overthrow.

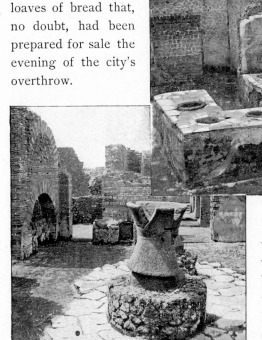

THE WINESHOP.

THE BAKERY.

Upon the outer walls of many of these buildings have been discovered notices, painted in red letters, urging the citizens to elect certain men to municipal offices. One of them reads as follows: "The carpenters recommend Marcellus for the post of Ædile." Is it possible then that Pompeii, also, had its Knights of Labor and its Walking Delegates? Perhaps Vesuvius did not do so bad a thing after all.

Another interesting mural souvenir of the buried city is the

A COLLECTION OF DISCOVERIES.

Greek alphabet rudely scratched upon the side of a house. The youthful student must have been a little fellow, for his hand formed the letters only about three feet above the ground. Two other walls are marked, respectively, with short quotations from Virgil and from Ovid, possibly written by children on their way to school.

The fascination of Pompeii appeals to every one. The Arch of Constantine, the columns of the Forum, and the temples at Pæstum appeal particularly only to the archæologist and scholar; but there is a pathetic, human realism in the excavated streets and buildings of Pompeii that moves the peasant no less deeply than the prince, and places the historian and the

HALL OF SMALL BRONZES.

thoughtless tourist upon practically the same ground. Most of the world's great architectural monuments, that by their massive strength have managed to survive the ravages of barbarism and the wrecks of time, are structures which their builders planned to last for centuries. Hence, while they call forth admiration, they stimulate the intellect alone, and never touch the heart. Pompeii, on the contrary, has a power to excite emotions such as no other city of antiquity can evoke, since it reveals to us in its minute details a life which, although separated from us by a gap of centuries, is not essentially different from our own. The objects found here are in one sense trivial, but they suggest the every-day existence of the human race. The tables spread with food, the loaves of bread in the oven,

THE TEMPLE OF ISIS.

the advertisements of theatrical entertainments, the instruments of toil, and articles of personal adornment bring us immediately in sympathetic contact with the occupations, joys, and sorrows of the men and women of Pompeii, and thus enable us easily to put ourselves in their places, and see how we should probably have lived and loved, said prayers to Isis and amused ourselves in the amphitheatre, had we been in their place on that bright and cloudless day when the terrific action of Vesuvius suddenly transformed this gay, noisy city into a silent sepulchre, and rolled a lava tombstone over it, there to remain for eighteen hundred years.

The Pompeian temple of Isis, although small, must have been very beautiful; for its remaining columns are still richly colored, and its walls were formerly covered with fine frescos. The marble altar in the centre seems waiting, even now, for its former fragrant offerings of incense; but no more worshipers will ever come to it while Time endures. Pompeii has awakened from her sleep of centuries to find her old religion superseded, her temples ruined, and her gods dethroned.

THE FORUM AND VESUVIUS.

The most pathetic fact connected with this shrine of Isis is the finding of a number of skeletons within its private sanctuary, accessible only to the priests, proving that some unhappy people had dared at last to enter even that most hallowed area, hoping Isis would at least spread over this, her special home, a mantle of protection. How miserably they must have died, while the light failed them steadily and surely, and, as they prayed in the stifling atmosphere, their voices grew fainter one by one, and finally were hushed in death! They probably met their fate, believing that the awful night, predicted by their poets, had at last arrived, when the world and the gods were to be destroyed together.

Turning from this temple, a few steps brought us to the Forum of Pompeii. This business centre of the city was

undergoing res-
toration at the
time of the erup-
tion, for it had
been injured by
an earthquake
shock sixteen
years before. It
should always be
remembered that
Pompeii was not
at its best when
the Vesuvian
ashes buried it.
Some of its public

THE COURT OF JUSTICE.

buildings had been utterly destroyed, and others partially ruined
by the previous calamity. Thus, in this Forum, all the columns
were still unfinished, and the pedestals were as yet without
their stat-   ues. Moreover, in the period of its
great-   est prosperity, Pompeii was
not   a prominent city of the
Roman Empire, but
merely ranked among
the third-class towns,
since it had only
thirty thousand in-
habitants. What,
therefore, must have
been the splendor
of the larger Roman
cities, when even
this small town has
revealed, in the mere
fragment of it thus

THE TRAGIC THEATRE.

far brought to
light, hundreds of
bronze and marble
statues, exquisite
paintings and mo-
saics, two forums,
eight temples, a
court of justice,
and two theatres,
besides an amphi-
theatre with a
seating capacity
for twenty thou-
sand people! Its
principal theatre
is wonderfully

A COLLECTION OF SCULPTURES.

well preserved, considering that it was completed long before the
birth of Christ. Five thousand people could be seated here. We
visited with the greatest interest its orchestra and stage, observed
the opening for the curtain, saw the dressing-rooms of the actors,
and, finally, climbed to the highest story and touched the ancient
rings which held the awning drawn between the assembled audience and the sun. Among
the seats of this theatre
were found sev-
eral of the num-
bered checks,
which ushers
used to take
when they con-
ducted people
to their places.
How near this
building brings

ARCH AND PAVEMENT.

us to a life, which, so many centuries ago, craved entertainment
and dramatic art as does our own, and found a means of satisfy-
ing this desire by methods not dissimilar.

Dramatic and spectacular performances were, evidently, very
popular in Pompeii. Upon the street walls have been found
advertisements of entertainments in the theatres and the amphitheatre. One of them reads as follows: "Thirty pairs of
gladiators will contend to-morrow at sunrise in the amphitheatre." Another
states : " A troop
of gladiators will
fight in Pompeii
on the last day
of June. There
will be a hunt."
When Roman
managers pre-
pared a "hunt,"
they planted trees
in the arena to
imitate a forest,
and, on the ap-
pointed day, let
loose among the
trees two or three

THE AMPHITHEATRE AT POMPEII.

lions, half a dozen tigers, an elephant, a boa-constrictor, and a
crocodile. Ten men were then obliged to enter the "forest"
and attack these animals. This was the kind of sport most dear
to the old Roman world, for it was even more exciting than a
gladiatorial fight. Every one knew how the latter must end.
The wounded man would, of course, fall at last, with more or
less grace, and receive the fatal blow; and it was usually understood between the gladiators that they would spare each other
all unnecessary suffering. With wild beasts, however, nothing

THE ERUPTION.

could be foretold. They would fight desperately to the last with tooth and claw. No graceful posturing was probable in those encounters. A wounded lion has no thought of the spectators. A maddened tiger shows no mercy. Accordingly, if a man here let his head swim, his hand fall, or his heart falter, he was instantly struck down and torn to pieces. Such scenes of bloodshed are too revolting to describe, yet from these very benches thousands beheld such sights, and these walls, which now will echo marvelously to the softest word, many a time resounded to roars of furious monsters and groans of dying men.

THE FLIGHT FROM POMPEII.

According to the historian, Dion Cassius, this building, at the time of the eruption, was filled with people, gazing no doubt with bated breath into the dust and blood of the arena, or yelling fiercely at some gladiator's stroke; but, suddenly, the animals refused to fight and made so great an uproar in the dens below that the astonished populace turned their gaze from the arena to the darkening sky, and there beheld the awful declaration of their doom. Think of the fear that must have suddenly blanched every cheek and caused the gladiator's arm to fall, when from that peaceful dome rushed forth the fiery elements of death! Without any warning, a column of smoke burst from the overhanging mountain, and rose to a prodigious height in the clear autumn

THE TEMPLE OF VENUS.

sky. There it gradually expanded in the form of a gigantic pine tree, till it hid the sun, and cast a shadow over the earth for miles. The people in the houses of the city were equally unprepared. Up to the moment of the eruption, that fifth day[1]

[1] The generally accepted date of the catastrophe has been August 24, A.D. 79, but November 5th is mentioned in one ancient manuscript as the time of the eruption, and the historian, Dion Cassius, also, says that it took place in the autumn. The discovery in the ruins of fruits and nuts which botanists state positively do not ripen till November, and could not have been there had the city been destroyed in August, confirms the probability that the later date is the correct one.

of November, in the year 79, had been beautiful, and the sky cloudless. Vesuvius looked down peacefully upon the lovely shore which it was soon to devastate, even more tranquil in appearance than it is to-day, as no smoke then emerged from its destruction-breathing cone. Nothing was feared from it, for it had not exhibited any signs of activity within the memory of man, and its smooth, cultivated slopes spoke only of fertility. The dreadful suddenness of the calamity is proved by the fact

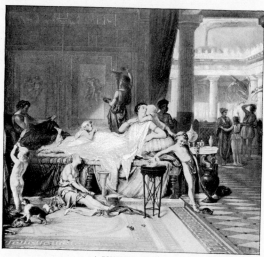

A POMPEIAN FAMILY.

that in the houses almost everything has been discovered in its accustomed place. Bread was in the ovens, and meat and fowl were half cooked. In one mansion, a dining-table was found covered with petrified dishes and surrounded by bronze couches, the occupants of which had, doubtless, risen from their banquet to struggle for their lives. The darkness speedily deepened into the blackness of night, illumined only by terrific lightning from the sulphurous clouds. Soon a thick shower of ashes fell to the depth of about three feet. Then came a rain of hot pumice-stones, seven or eight feet deep, setting the city in a blaze of fire. Meanwhile the earth rocked with repeated shocks, and through the thick and suffocating air resounded peals of thunder, like salvos of artillery from the walls of heaven. Even those who finally reached a place of safety were nearly dead from terror and exhaustion.

NYDIA.

Perhaps the most successful historical novel ever written is Bulwer's "Last Days of Pompeii." Its incidents come back to us at every step; and, in imagination, we trace the pathway of the blind girl — Nydia — who, in the dreadful darkness that prevailed, was by means of her very infirmity able to find her way, and thus conduct her lover — Glaucus — to the sea. How marvelous is the power of a skillful novelist! As London is forever peopled for us with the characters of Dickens, so are Pompeii's silent streets made real to us by our remembrance of Arbaces, Glaucus, Nydia and Ione. That Bulwer's fiction is, however, no exaggeration of the terrible reality, we can be easily convinced by looking on the bodies which have been discovered in the ruins.

It is evident that there came a time when flight was no longer possible. Those who had taken refuge in their cellars were destined to remain there until liberated by

CAST OF MOTHER AND DAUGHTER.

explorers in the nineteenth century. If any emerged, they were struck down by red-hot stones, or suffocated by the whirling ashes. Thus, panting for breath, groping in the darkness, not knowing where to turn, and blocked by the piles of pumice-stones which had been falling steadily for hours, and had already reached the windows of the first floors of their houses, they soon fell prostrate, and were buried in the constantly increasing mass. The most of those who perished probably lingered too long, in order to secure their property. Beside one woman's body, for example, were found two heavy bracelets, several rings of gold, and a well-filled purse. Another body discovered in Pompeii is that of an old man around whose waist is the mark of a money-belt containing gold and jewels, the efforts to secure which probably cost him his life.

There is a singular fascination in thinking of the possible history of these Pompeian dead. Had this unfortunate man a wife and children who, having reached some place of safety, waited for his coming, hour after hour, until hope died within their breasts? Or, had they previously perished, and was he finally seeking to escape by himself, not caring in his desolate

BODY OF AN OLD MAN.

POMPEII.

bereavement what might become his fate? We cannot tell.
All that we know is that his body was discovered here alone.
Still more pathetic was the finding of four bodies, evidently
those of prisoners, whose feet were fastened in iron stocks, the
lock of which had held them fast. Close by them, but beyond
their reach, lay the key that might have freed them, which was
doubtless dropped by the jailer as he fled for life, oblivious of
his captives, or
deaf to their ap-
peals.

HOUSE OF DIOMEDE.

In one of the
excavated houses,
known as the
Villa of Diomede,
were unearthed
the skeletons of
seventeen persons
who had sought
refuge in the cel-
lar, providing
themselves with
food and drink,
and thinking,
doubtless, that
the tempest would soon cease. It was a fatal mistake. Little by
little the ashes crept in after them, and, having stifled them with
poisonous fumes, wove deftly around them a sepulchral shroud
which was to last for ages. Two of them, apparently the master
and a slave, evidently made at last a desperate effort to escape,
for their bodies were found near the garden gate, and beside
them were several caskets of jewels and the keys of the mansion, the only objects taken with them in their flight.

Leaving this villa we entered the Street of Tombs, or the
burial-place of those who died before the city's overthrow.

THE STREET OF TOMBS.

How strange to think that this was once the only street of the dead within Pompeii! Now all the others have become so too, and, thus far, about six hundred and fifty corpses have been found in them. In front of one of these tombs the workmen came upon the bodies of a woman and three children, locked in one another's arms. Perhaps, that November afternoon, they had been paying a visit to the grave of husband and father; or, possibly, they fled here in their terror, seeking instinctively, in spite of death, help from the one who had in life protected them. In this street, also, was discovered the body of a dog which seems to have died in agony. As it lay near the form of a man it is not unreasonable to suppose that the poor creature had refused to leave his master, and

THE DOG.

hence perished with him, for otherwise there seems to be no reason why he should not have escaped. If so, immortalized in this
his mantle of destruction, he is a touching symbol of that wonderful fidelity which has been shown so many times by man's most
faithful and devoted friend. There was philosophy as well as wit
in the epigram, "The more I know men, the more I admire dogs."

But the most touching proof of fidelity and affection was
a discovery made in the building known as the House of the
Faun. In a niche,
overlooking the
garden, was found
the skeleton of a
dove which —
throughout all the
thunder, light-
ning, darkness,
noise, and suffo-
cating shower of
hot ashes of that
dreadful scene —
had remained
crouched upon
her nest, faithful

HALL OF LARGE BRONZES.

to death in guarding there the egg which, after eighteen centuries, was found beneath her, still holding the tiny bones of
her embryo offspring.

"But," it may be asked, "how were these bodies thus preserved for centuries?" In a literal sense they have not been
preserved, and yet their forms are reproduced with absolute
fidelity. The destruction of Pompeii was accomplished by two
distinct agencies: first, by the showers of hot pumice-stones;
and, secondly, by the streams of mud descending from Vesuvius. The former were so light that they lay loosely round the
substances they buried, and often did not break or injure in the

slightest degree objects composed even of glass, and, much less, articles of ivory or metal. The volcanic mud, on the contrary, as it hardened, formed round the object it enclosed a perfect mold. Accordingly, Signor Fiorelli, the director of the excavations at Pompeii, conceived the happy idea of pouring liquid plaster into the hollows formed by molds containing human bones, and thus obtained casts of the dead, which show not only the form and features, but also the very attitude in which the victims of Vesuvius met their fate. Some seem to have died without a struggle; while others, by their clinched hands, arms raised to ward off the descending ashes, and limbs drawn up convulsively, evidently struggled desperately to the last.

Before departing from Pompeii we spent some time in watching the work of excavation. It is a fascinating yet a melancholy sight; fascinating, because at any moment the pick or shovel may disclose new treasures; but sad, because the progress is so slow that we shall probably never know half that is hidden under all the earth still waiting to be turned to the light of day. It makes one wish that the United States could own Pompeii for about six months. The Italian Govern-

EXCAVATIONS AT POMPEII.

THE SITE OF TASSO'S HOUSE, SORRENTO.

THE ROAD TO AMALFI.

ment sets aside for excavations here only twelve thousand dollars a year, and at the present rate sixty years more will be required to unearth the city. Not in exaggeration, but sober earnest do I say that, were Pompeii within our territory, the whole sum needed could be raised easily within a week among the public-spirited citizens of this Republic, and within half a year the whole remaining portion of Pompeii would be laid open to the scholars of the world. What would three-quarters of a million be to raise for such a purpose when one American gives a million dollars for the founding of an art museum?

The road beyond Pompeii, on the southern shore toward Sorrento and Amalfi, is one of the finest in the world. For miles it

ATRANI.

winds through pretty towns and over vine-clad terraces, sometimes upon a shelf of rock hundreds of feet above the
waves. Beside it countless orange and lemon trees hang out
their golden globes against the clear blue sky, and the soft
breeze which passes over them conveys the perfume of a million blossoms to the sea. Occasionally, also, on high bluffs
appear the threatening forms of ruined castles which, in the
distance, look like outgrowths of the cliffs themselves, and
seem as truly portions of the crags on which they stand as
were the fabled centaur's head and shoulders a part of the
steed from which they sprang. They serve as reminders of the
fact that, formerly, this coast was lined with massive towers
whose bells gave warning of the approach of pirates. Best of
all, beneath us always on this glorious driveway is the sparkling
sea. It knows no change amid these ruins of the
past, but spreads along the shore its filagree of silver
foam, as when its waves were fur-
rowed by the
ships from Troy.

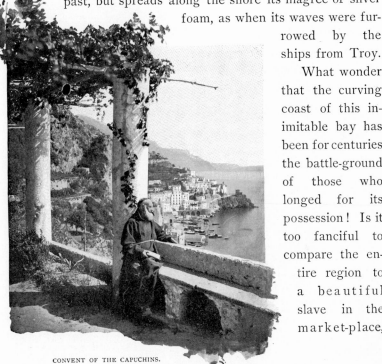

What wonder
that the curving
coast of this in-
imitable bay has
been for centuries
the battle-ground
of those who
longed for its
possession! Is it
too fanciful to
compare the en-
tire region to
a beautiful
slave in the
market-place,

CONVENT OF THE CAPUCHINS.

SORRENTO.

contended for by wrangling rivals, who have in turn possessed, ill-treated, and abandoned her, till now her smile, though beautiful and bewitching as of old, has for the traveler who knows her history a sadness which is full of pathos? Greeks, Romans, Norsemen, Saracens,

FISHING-BOATS.

Frenchmen, and Spaniards all fought desperately to secure her; but, one by one, her masters became enervated by her charms, and the strong hand that grasped the sword at first so firmly, gradually relaxed its hold, and, finally, did little save bestow caresses till a new conqueror arrived.

Now and then a turn in the road reveals to us a score of fishermen's boats along the beach. "Is it possible," we cry, "that these patched, dingy sails are such as we admire far out upon the bay, as the boats glide with snow-white wings from Ischia to Capri?" Ah! but the poet tells us:

"The sails we see on the ocean
  Are as white, as white can be;
But never one in the harbor
  Is as white as the sails at sea.

Yet, Distance, thou dear enchantress,
  Still hold in thy magic veil
The glory of far-off mountains,
  The gleam of the far-off sail."

After a drive of several hours through enchanting scenery we reached the village of Amalfi. I can hardly imagine a more picturesque situation than this town possesses. Behind it, frowning cliffs rise perpendicularly from the sea; and on these, perched at dizzy heights, are hundreds of dwellings, tier above tier, as if a hurricane had blown them there, and a slight earthquake shock might send them tumbling off the ledges like an avalanche of stones. Incredible though it seems, Amalfi was, eight hundred years ago, a prominent commercial city, and the centre of a powerful republic which vied with Genoa and Pisa, made laws that governed the Mediterranean, from the Rock of Gibraltar to the Golden Horn, and founded colonies even in Africa and Asia. But now Amalfi lies upon

AMALFI.

THE PLEASURES OF THE CHASE.

the shore, like the frail remnant of a vessel cast upon the rocks, and hardly a vestige of its former grandeur remains; for Pisa conquered it at last, and earthquakes and invading waves have tried to finish what was thus begun. The present degenerate inhabitants of Amalfi are engaged principally in begging, and, incidentally, in manufacturing soap and macaroni. So far as my observation went, however, they are exceedingly partial in their use of these manufactured articles, — devouring

CASAMICCIOLA, ISCHIA, BEFORE THE EARTHQUAKE.

the macaroni with the keenest appetite, but carefully excluding soap from the list of articles for home consumption.

A jewel, rivaling even Capri in the gorgeous setting of the Bay of Naples, is the island of Ischia which, every year for centuries, has, siren-like, lured thousands of admirers to its sea-girt cliffs. Few islands in the world have been more famous for their beauty and enchanting situation than Ischia. Renan called

CASTLE OF ISCHIA.

it his "dear volcano,"
and every one who
knows it feels its charm.
Yet Ischia has been a pitiless enchantress, and her loveliness has proved a veritable magnet of misfortune; for it is
estimated that its earthquakes have destroyed, in all, no less than
seventy thousand people.   According to the poet Virgil the
island rests upon the rebellious giant Typhoëus who, ever and
anon writhing in agony, shakes the earth in his convulsive
efforts to throw off the crushing weight; but, notwithstanding
the long record of calamities caused by this restless monster,
such is the fascination of the view from Ischia, so healthful are
its mineral baths, and so delightful are its summer breezes, that
all its injured villages have been invariably rebuilt after an
earthquake, just as luxuriant vegetation comes again to hide
earth's scars beneath a mass of roses, and clothe the hills once
more with beauty and fertility.

There is something pathetic in the trust which human beings have in the goodness and immutability of Nature. No matter what may have been the world's upheavals in the past, men look up into the blue vault of heaven, or on the tranquil ground beneath their feet, and do not deem it possible that any more disasters can occur. Alas, how frequently they are deceived! For Nature, "red in tooth and claw," seems absolutely indifferent to human suffering and destruction; and nothing is more certain, as we trace the history of the race, than that millions of our fellow-beings have been destroyed, not only by wild beasts and reptiles, but by the ravages of natural forces,— cyclones, volcanoes, avalanches, tidal waves, and earthquakes.

In the summer of 1883 some twenty thousand people, heedless of danger or trusting confidently in the future, were living on this island of Ischia. Steamers brought hither hundreds of tourists daily, and on the night of the 28th of July the villas and hotels of the principal town of Ischia — Casamicciola — were filled with happy residents and guests. It was a beautiful

LA PICCOLA SENTINELLA.

evening.   The sea was calm, the air was balmy, the town was
bright with lights and gay with music.   How horrible to think
that just beneath this charming picture, underlying all the
little villas nestling in their rose gardens, the awful forces of
destruction were gathering to strike a deadly blow!   It was
half-past nine o'clock.   Dinner was over in the hotels.   Most
of the guests were strolling on the flowery terraces, enjoying
the refreshing coolness of the sea, and gazing with delight into
the starlit heavens, upon the ruddy glow above the crest of
Mount Vesuvius, or on the placid surface of the bay.   In the
hotel called *La Piccola Sentinella* an impromptu concert was
in progress.   An English gentleman was seated at the piano,
and, strangely enough, the piece he was playing was Chopin's
" Funeral March."   A Frenchman, shrugging his shoulders at
the lugubrious selection, left the room, and out of all that
company he alone was saved.

Suddenly the entire island shook convulsively.   The movement lasted only fifteen seconds; but when it was over a sweet,

CASAMICCIOLA DESTROYED.

DRAWING-ROOM OF LA PICCOLA, AFTER THE EARTHQUAKE.

peaceful scene of human happiness and industry had been
transformed into one of agony and ruin. The walls and roof
of *La Piccola Sentinella* had fallen like a house of cards, bury-
ing all the company in the *débris*. The " Funeral March " had
ushered in a carnival of death. Soft happy voices either had
been stilled forever, or were now heard in shrieks of anguish;
the pure air, laden with the perfume of flowers and the breath
of the sea, was choked with stifling clouds of dust; and, here
and there, streams of burning oil from overturned lamps ran
like the tongues of devils through the entangled timbers and
threatened the imprisoned victims with the worst of deaths.
When the drawing-room of the hotel was subsequently excavated, the dead pianist was found still seated before the crushed
piano, and a girl who had just sung to his accompaniment
lay dead beside him. Not a house in Casamicciola was left

THE RUINS.

standing; and its streets and lovely gardens were filled with
shattered buildings, pianos, statues, pictures, and household
furniture heaped up in broken fragments, and forming a horrible chaos.

Buildings were tossed about, as if their walls had possessed
no more strength than paper screens. In all, more than two
thousand persons either perished on the spot, or subsequently
starved to death in situations from which they could not be
extricated. The night that followed was one of the most terrible recorded in even the appalling history of the Bay of
Naples. Groping in darkness, the horrified survivors crawled
over the *débris*, while the groans of the dying, the shrieks of
the suffering, and the appeals of the terror-stricken came up
to them through the crevices from the living tombs below.

When the morning dawned, soldiers had arrived to work
among the ruins, and steamers brought out to the island, every

hour, cargoes of food, beds, medicine, and coffins. But half of
the population of Casamicciola was either dead or buried alive.
Sometimes a hand was seen emerging piteously from a mass of
stones, as if the wrist were held in a vice. What was below
it no one dared to think. Meantime, the lamentations and
delirious excitement of the rescued, whose husbands, wives,
children, or sweethearts were heard moaning faintly or implor-
ing help, can be imagined; especially when one considers the
emotional nature of the Neapolitans. It is said that King
Humbert, who went at once to the scene of the disaster, exclaimed, as the tears rolled down his face, " My God! I never
dreamed of such misery as this."

Think, indeed, of the horror of regaining consciousness, to
find yourself held down by beams or masonry, a portion of
your body crushed, bruised, or broken, and some one very
dear to you lying dead beside you; or, still worse, suffering and
calling for help beyond your reach! There were some wonderful instances of preservation and rescue. Two ladies, for

WHERE THE DEAD LAY.

example, found themselves lying under an iron girder which had fallen in such a way as just to protect them from a mass of masonry ten feet thick. They were imprisoned thus for sixty-seven hours, but were finally saved unharmed. An American lady was found with her feet crushed, while a huge beam hung trembling above her, like the sword of Damocles; but, although released from her terrible position, she lived only eight days.

The most prominent feature of the island of Ischia is Monte Epomeo, a mountain rising twenty-six hundred feet above the sea. It is a volcano which, until Vesuvius resumed activity in the early part of the Christian era, appeared to be the safety-valve for the volcanic agencies at work around the Bay of Naples; but as it has not poured out any lava since 1302, scientists consider it now to be extinct and harmless. Still, when one thinks that the destruction of Pompeii was occasioned by

MONTE EPOMEO.

CAPRI ROCKS.

LOOKING TOWARD CAPRI.

a mountain also supposed to be entirely tranquil, he is unable
to feel perfectly secure at Ischia.

On one side Monte Epomeo rises abruptly from the sea, but
toward the centre of the island its slopes are carefully cultivated and the whole country, from the level of the shore up
to the shoulders of the mountain, has been transformed into
a vast garden of olives, cherries, lemons, figs, and vines. The
view from the summit is unspeakably glorious; and, considering
the beauty of the islands, sea, and shore, and the historic associations which enrich them, the series of magnificent curves
which the Italian coast spreads out beneath the traveler's eyes,
through a radius of fifty miles from Mount Vesuvius, has not
its equal in the world, save, possibly, the view from Mount
Pentelicus in Greece.

I shall never forget an afternoon spent on the slopes of

Monte Epomeo.   Nothing
disturbed my reverie and
all the subtle fascination
which the historic element
in scenery
exerts, when
linked with

THE "MATCHLESS BAY."

natural beauty, held
me for hours a willing
captive; and, as I
looked off from my book upon
the classic sea, over whose surface distant sails were gliding slowly toward
the setting sun, I felt that I was drinking
deeply of a joy which might in after years prove a most potent
opiate for care and sorrow.   It was as sweet an hour as was
ever numbered on the rosary of Time.   Even when I had finally
begun the descent to Casamicciola, I paused repeatedly to look
back upon the enchanting scene.   The sun was setting behind
Capri, which lay in rose and crimson splendor on the surface of
the ocean, like an emperor's barge.   Above it, in a blaze of
glory, the cloud-fleets spread their magic sails, and threw their
radiant pennants to the breeze, as if to follow in the track of the

departing sun. Strange legends seemed to glitter on those sails and banners, as if the annals of the matchless bay had been inscribed upon them; and I stood spellbound watching them, in perfect sympathy with the associations of the place, until at last the solar fires burnt themselves out, and left on the horizon nothing but the pale gray ashes of twilight, beneath which the aërial ships had vanished like a dream.

More interesting even than Ischia, and certainly far safer as a place of residence, is the island of Capri on the other side of the bay. This, seen at any time, either when gilded by the dawn, mantled in purple by the sunset light, or turned to silver by the moon, is wonderfully beautiful. Moreover, few spots on earth can boast of more historic memories. This home of the Sirens became the home of the Cæsars. The Emperor Augustus was extremely fond of Capri, and made of it a bower of delight. The poet Virgil, therefore, and his sovereign lived then directly opposite each other across the bay, — the poet at Posilipo, the Emperor at Capri. When Augustus died, this

THE HEADLAND, CAPRI.

island was bequeathed by him to his successor, Tiberius, who, when he felt the end of his life approaching, came to this sea-girt rock, in the twenty-sixth year of the Christian era, as a wounded beast crawls into a cave to die. Acting, however, as if he were to live indefinitely, he built upon these cliffs twelve splendid villas, each vying with its neighbor in magnificence, and all of them adorned with theatres, statues, groves, and gardens. In each of these palaces he lived a month, in turn, throughout the year, making this island for a time the centre of the civilized world, whence by a word or gesture he could spread terror through an empire extending from the moors of Scotland to the cataracts of the Nile. Of the imperial abodes which once stood forth above the jeweled water of the bay, like tinted alabaster in the setting sun, scarcely a trace remains; but eighteen hundred years have not effaced the memory of Tiberius. He is the evil genius of the place. Historians relate almost incredible stories of his cruelties and debaucheries. How sad this termination to a youth of promise! As a young man he was a famous general, a skilled diplomat, and a prudent

THE LANDING-PLACE.

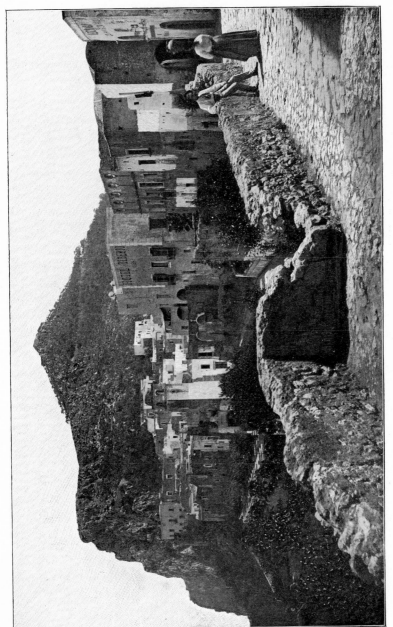

HOTEL TIBERIUS, CAPRI.

THE VILLA OF TIBERIUS.

governor; but supreme power, with its attendant risks and cares, gave him a haunting dread of being murdered, inclining him to orgies of unutterable dissipation, varied by outbursts of inhuman cruelty. What a significant fact it is that while this hated sovereign was living here, in shameless infamy, in one of the obscurest corners of his empire Jesus died upon the Cross! Moreover, it was here that Tiberius heard of the Crucifixion, if at all, from the Judean Governor, Pilate.

Bearing these facts in mind, we climbed to the summit of the Capriot cliff which most precipitously overhangs the sea. Here, formerly, stood one of the imperial villas; and the appalling precipice, nearly one

THE "LEAP OF TIBERIUS."

thousand feet in height, is still known as the " Leap of Tiberius,"
because from this, it is said, he used to have his victims hurled
after protracted tortures ; while, lest by any possibility they
might survive, sailors were stationed below, to beat the mangled
bodies until life became extinct.   What a spectacle for men and
gods to look upon was that of this miserable master of the world,
pale from debauchery and haunted with insomnia, standing upon
this cliff, with the unspeakable glory of the bay, from Baiæ to

THE STEAMER AT CAPRI.

Sorrento, here outspread before him, yet finding his enjoyment
in watching tortured men hurled downward to the sea!

As all the world knows, the most attractive natural feature
of Capri is its wonderful Blue Grotto.   On every pleasant day,
a little steamer brings tourists here from Naples and Sorrento,
and, as soon as it has halted, a score of boats dart forward,
buzzing and circling about, like honey bees attacking a sweet
flower.   These boats are of necessity very small.   Only two
passengers beside the boatman are allowed in each of them,
and even though the party be but three in number, it must be
divided.   In the Blue Grotto, as in other places in this world,
" Two are company, three are a crowd."   The cause of this is
obvious, for the opening to the grotto is so small that one who

THE BLUE GROTTO.

does not know its situation looks for it in vain. Even when found, the tourists' boats slip through the aperture like coins dropping into a purse. In fact, unless the sea be calm and the wind favorable, the traveler cannot enter it at all. It seemed to me as I approached, that, with a little assistance from a rising wave, I might easily crack my skull like an egg-shell on the rock. I therefore gladly obeyed the order to lie down. For a few moments I looked up tranquilly at the sky; then I could feel that the boat was rising on a little wave; it suddenly shot forward; one instant, and the entire mountain seemed to be falling on my breast; the next we were within a fairy place. I started up with exclamations of delight. Walls, roof, and water had assumed a color such as no painter in the world can reproduce. In truth, it did not seem like water, but, rather, like

THE BOATS AT CAPRI.

folds of shimmering blue satin, moving around and beneath us in luminous, transparent waves. The submerged oar seemed a blade of sapphire. My hand, when dipped in the marvelous liquid, gleamed like silver. Out toward the bay the tiny opening, through which alone the light can enter, appeared like the sun emerging from a sea of turquoises. The silence of the place is, also, most impressive. Outside, the waves may dash against the cliffs; but here, beneath a dome, apparently of lapis-lazuli, the ocean seems astonished at its sudden transformation, and holds its breath, enamoured of its own unlooked-for beauty. It is not well, however, to linger too long in the Blue Grotto. If the sea becomes violent and barricades the portal with a watery wall, an exit is impossible, and visitors must wait till the wind changes and the waves go down. Travelers who have come to spend twenty minutes here have sometimes been detained twenty-four hours. In doubtful weather, therefore, the boatmen from Sorrento usually carry food with them for such an emergency. A passageway, long since filled up, used to connect this ocean cavern with the cliffs above; and it is possible that Tiberius kept the grotto as a place of refuge, and as a secret exit from the island to the outer world.

Among my most delightful memories of travel, I treasure that of a sail across the bay from Capri to Naples by moonlight. For hours everything lulled us to complete oblivion of care and

THE NATURAL ARCH.

SAILING FROM CAPRI.

calm enjoyment of the present. As our boat bent her cheek
to the waves, the water answered the caressing movement
with a sound resembling a sigh. Occasionally, white-winged
vessels glided by us, ghost-like on their way to Sicily, meeting the wavelets from the outer sea, which, having passed the
isle of Capri, seemed to have been turned into molten silver
by the moon. Before us rose the fire-crowned volcano, emitting
smoke and flames as from a sacrificial altar which has claimed
its many victims. Enraptured by the scene, I felt that I could
linger here, as heedless of the lapse of time as was the monk
who laid his ear so close to heaven that he heard in his dreams
the music of Paradise, and woke to find he had been listening
to it for a thousand years. On that night, therefore, I realized
as never before the truth and exquisite beauty of the lines:

> " My soul to-day
> Is far away,
> Sailing the blue Vesuvian bay,

With watchful eyes
My spirit lies
Under the walls of Paradise.

Far, vague, and dim
The mountains swim,
While on Vesuvius' misty brim,
With outstretched hands,
The gray smoke stands
O'erlooking the volcanic lands.

There Ischia smiles
O'er liquid miles,
And yonder — bluest of the isles —
Calm Capri waits,
Her sapphire gates
Beguiling to her bright estates.

No more, no more
The worldly shore
Upbraids me with its loud uproar.
With dreamful eyes
My spirit lies
Under the walls of Paradise."

ROME

ROME

IT would be easier to write ten lectures upon Rome than one. The supreme difficulty is: first, to choose what is essential to even an approximately thorough delineation of the Eternal City, and then to treat of it in words which shall not be so brief as to suggest a catalogue of names. Ancient, mediæval, papal, ecclesiastical, artistic, and modern Rome are the fewest divisions possible for any genuine study of the subject, and these can be subdivided almost indefinitely. A single lecture, therefore, on so vast a theme must of necessity be fragmentary; and whatever method be adopted to describe the Eternal City within the limits of a hundred and twenty pages, immeasurably more will be omitted than can be even mentioned. Still, as the rendering of a few selections from an opera may serve to stimulate the wish to hear it all, from the first

FATHER TIBER.

measure of the overture to the last strain of the finale, so it is hoped the following pages may awaken in anticipation, or revive in memory, something of the reverence and affection created in the writer by Eternal Rome — a reverence inspired by no other city upon earth — and an affection that has left no room for rivalry.

If every reader of these lines were requested to select the city which, could he choose but one, he would desire above all others to behold, I think there would be only one reply. It would be, — Rome. Whence comes this universal interest? Why should this ruined city of the Past prove more attractive than any other capital? The secret is not merely its antiquity. Athens is still more ancient, yet it possesses no such charm. It is not solely its relation to Christianity. Constantinople was for centuries the Eastern capital of the Christian church, in some respects more striking and magnificent than Rome ; and yet how small is the attraction of the Bosphorus compared to that which lures us to the Tiber! The cause is doubtless this : that,

THE MARBLE FAUN.

more than any spot on earth, Rome centres in itself the history of the race for twenty centuries. Absorbing by its universal conquests the fruits of all preceding civilizations and the treasures of all lands, it is, historically, the intellectual capital of the world. The current of continuous historic life flows through it now as surely and inevitably as the Tiber. Its modes of government, politics, art, jurisprudence, military science, and Church history have traveled further even than the Roman legions, till they have reached the confines of the globe. We are in many ways Rome's offspring. In every sentence that

ROME, FROM THE BALCONY OF ST. PETER'S.

POMPEY.

we speak, we use, perhaps unconsciously, some relics of her glorious language; much of our varied culture has come directly from her literature; and many of the laws which keep our social framework from disintegration were first promulgated beneath the arches of the Forum. Nor is this strange, for Rome was, what no other place has ever been, the one administrative centre of the world. All other capitals, however great, were in comparison petty and provincial. Rome only could be called in grand simplicity *Urbs* — the City.

Nothing stands out more prominently in my remembrance of Rome than the first morning after my arrival there. I had seen practically nothing on the previous night, between the railway station and my hotel, and the delightful consciousness of being actually in the City of the Cæsars had, therefore, wakened me at an early hour. Sleep was of course no longer possible, and pushing back the shutters I looked out. Beneath me was a square, still quite deserted at that morning hour, and from it rose a lofty column glistening in the sun. Winding around this, on a spiral path, I could discern a

THE COLUMN OF MARCUS AURELIUS.

THE TIBER.

multitude of figures in relief, portraying Roman soldiers and their conquests under Marcus Aurelius. Yet, when I leaned out of my window and viewed the column in its entirety, I saw that it was surmounted by a statue of St. Paul. "What a complete and comprehensive introduction to old Rome is this!" I murmured, "for my first glance embraces here proofs of the three great epochs in her history: an imperial monument, an apostolic statue, and a modern square. Yes, Pagan, Christian, Modern Rome, all these are now awaiting me beneath the bright, blue sky of Italy!"

Two hours later I started out upon my first and ever-memorable walk in Rome. My companion was a cultivated gentleman of middle life who, though he had lived longer in Rome than I had in the world, apparently took delight in acting as my guide, sharing and even stimulating my enthusiasm.

"I leave my course entirely to you," I said, as we emerged from the hotel, "where will you take me first?"

"There is but one appropriate place to lead you at the start," he answered, "most travelers seek at once some ruin of old Rome, forgetting that there is something older here than any work of man, — it is the Tiber."

When, a few moments later, we had reached it I understood why he had led me hither at the outset; for, amid all the changes that have swept over Rome, one thing at least remains unchanged. It is the yellow, legend-laden Tiber, still rolling on, like molten gold, beneath its arches toward the setting sun, and guarding in its tawny breast some of the mightiest memories of the world. How many lives it has remorselessly engulfed, from those of brave defenders of the city to countless victims of imperial tyranny! And oh, what treasures, statues, ornaments, and spoils of vanquished nations lurk within its sands! For this historic river has never been satisfactorily explored. The French once offered to divert its channel that they might seek beneath its present bed the objects which are no doubt lying there; but the authorities of Rome, fearing an increase of malaria from such excavations, would not give their consent.

Midway between the river's banks I recognized the Isola Tiberina, — the solitary island of the Tiber. It is still sharply pointed at one end, and one can understand why the old Romans compared it to a ship, the bow of which faced down the stream. Tradition states that to further carry out this likeness they built a wall around the entire island like the bulwarks of a ship, and erected an obelisk in the centre to represent a mast. However that may be, the narrow end at least of the Isola Tiberina was certainly fashioned like a prow; and there, carved on a block of the old wall constructed twenty centuries ago, my comrade

THE ISLAND.

pointed out to me a portion of the symbolic staff of Æsculapius encircled by a serpent. How far back into antiquity that bit of sculpture carries the imagination! Nearly three hundred years before the Christian era a plague was devastating Rome, and messengers were sent to Greece to bring thence to the afflicted city a statue of Æsculapius, the god of medicine. They were successful in obtaining it, but when their returning ship was sailing up the Tiber a serpent, the emblem of Æsculapius, glided from it and landed on the island. The Romans hailed the omen with delight, and built upon the spot a temple, which is mentioned by the writers of antiquity, but has now completely disappeared;

ÆSCULAPIUS.

destroyed perhaps by a thunderbolt of Jupiter who, according to mythology, is said to have thus killed Æsculapius himself, because, forsooth, Pluto had complained that on account of his cures Hades was fast becoming depopulated!

STATUE OF GARIBALDI, AND DOME OF ST. PETER'S.

"The bridge upon your right," remarked my friend, "connecting the island with the mainland, is the famous Pons Fabricius, erected here nearly a century before Christ to replace a still more ancient bridge of wood; and you remember the poet,

Horace, speaks of it as a favorite place for those who wished to commit suicide by drowning."

"You mean, of course," I said, "that this bridge is a successor of the ancient one on the same site?"

"No, no," was his reply, "these very arches spanned the Tiber in the days of Cæsar, and part of the original inscription is still visible."

What grand conceptions of their future greatness and the permanency of their city the old Romans had when they made roads, built bridges, and erected edifices! Thus, when the re-

ARCH OF DRUSUS.

cent entry of the railroad into Rome made necessary the destruction of a part of the old wall, built by King Servius Tullius five hundred and sixty-four years before the Christian era, it still remained so solid after two thousand four hundred years that powder had to be used to blow it into fragments. It is significant, also, that the title of one of the oldest and most important of Roman officials was that of Pontifex, which meant, originally, "bridge builder"; and to be Pontifex Maximus was an honor that gave additional glory even to a Roman emperor.

A still more wonderful illustration of the strength and durability of Roman architecture is furnished by the Cloaca Maxima, or principal sewer of the ancient city. Pliny, who wrote in the first century of the Christian era, spoke with unqualified admiration of this monstrous conduit, and marveled that such a "monument of antiquity," as he called it, should be in existence after the earthquakes,

THE CLOACA MAXIMA.

accidents, and use of nearly seven hundred years. But what would his astonishment have been could he have known that one thousand eight hundred years after his time the huge stone sewer would still be in use, and that its massive, un-

THE CLOACA MAXIMA, IN THE FORUM.

cemented arch would be, apparently, as strong in the nineteenth century after Christ as in the sixth century before Him! I know of nothing which so reveals the magnitude of the ideas and plans that governed the establishment of Rome

as the provisions for the drainage of the city, which were
on such a colossal scale as to satisfy completely the needs
of Rome, both in the time of the Empire with its enormous water supply and in these modern times. Will any
government contractor of the present century leave such a
memorial as this? Turning a few steps from the river we
approached a little circular structure, whose ugly, modern roof
appeared entirely out of keeping with its twenty beautiful
Corinthian col-
umns.

THE TEMPLE OF VESTA AND THE TIBER.

"Surely," I
said (anxious to
show my knowl-
edge of the city),
"surely I recog-
nize this from
pictures I have
seen of it, it is the
Temple of Vesta."

My comrade
smiled. "Be not
too sure of that,"
he answered,
"some scholars
it is true still call
it so, but the majority claim that it is a Temple of Hercules."

"Whichever it may be," I said, "what most surprises me is,
that so frail a structure still survives when many larger buildings have gone down in ruin."

"The secret of its preservation," said my friend, "is this,
that over it the Church for ages spread its mantle of protection, since it was early used as a place of Christian worship."

The Vestals are among the most interesting personages of
the old Roman world. They were only six in number, and of

THE TEMPLE OF VESTA.

a great variety in age, a child under ten years being always chosen to fill a vacancy caused by death or by the retirement of a priestess, which was obligatory at the age of forty. These virgin priestesses, like the nuns of the Roman Catholic Church, took a vow of chastity, but of poverty and obedience they knew comparatively nothing. That they lived in almost regal splendor, is proved by the magnificent House of the Vestals discovered, in 1883, upon the Palatine; for it evidently was sumptuously furnished, and had spacious courts, fine columns, beautiful mosaic pavements, apartments lined with precious marble, and a large number of statues (chiefly portraits of distinguished Vestals), together with all the appliances for comfort known to wealthy Romans, including luxurious bath-rooms and flues in the walls for heating with hot air. Far from being rigidly bound to obedience, no women in Rome enjoyed such independence as the Vestal Virgins. They were

THE HOUSE OF THE VESTALS.

not held amenable to the common law, being subject only to the
Pontifex Maximus, who exercised over them an authority more
nominal than real. Their privileges, too, exceeded those of the
Roman matrons, since they alone had the right of holding
property and making wills, while others of their sex were
obliged to consider in such matters their fathers or their husbands. Moreover, they were allowed to drive in the streets of
Rome, while other ladies were conveyed in sedan-chairs, and when

they thus ap-
peared in public,
a lictor made the
crowd fall back
to let them pass.
In all important
ceremonies, too,
these white-robed
virgins took pre-
cedence even of
the Consuls, and
in the public
places of amuse-
ment not only
were the choicest
seats reserved
for them, but by

A STREET IN OLD ROME.

a decree of the Senate the Empress, when in public, was
obliged to sit with them. Such was the reverence felt for
them, that if a condemned criminal, on his way to execution,
met a Vestal he was immediately set at liberty. All these
advantages were theirs on two conditions: that of maintain-
ing constantly the sacred fire in the temple of Vesta, and of
adhering faithfully to their vow of chastity. A Vestal whose
neglect allowed the sacred fire to be extinguished was liable
to be scourged by the Pontifex Maximus; and any priestess

guilty of unchastity received the awful punishment of being
buried alive. A frightful dungeon was reserved for her, and
into this the unhappy woman was lowered with her infant
child, to be encased in walls that never opened until slow starvation had fulfilled its task. Nor was this punishment then deemed
too severe ; for, in the early days of Rome, when morals were
austere and justice prompt of execution, the fire kept forever
burning by the Vestals was emblematic of social purity. To

ON THE PINCIAN HILL.

break their vow of
chastity was, there-
fore, sacrilege;
since in the minds
of all the virtue of
a Vestal stood as
a model for the
nation.

Calling a cab
at this point, we
drove to the sum-
mit of the Pincian
Hill, the beautiful
public promenade
of Rome, laid out
in   charming
avenues and paths,
about which scores of busts and statues of distinguished Romans
stand out against a background of dark pines and cypresses,
and hint to us that, back of all the brilliant Present here, there
lies the grandeur of a mighty Past.   In truth, this famous
esplanade is like a stage devoted alternately to comedy and
tragedy.   On pleasant afternoons it is a scene of fashion and
frivolity. A multitude of people then invades the place, and
the occupants of the many carriages which roll along its flower-
bordered avenues converse, bow, smile, and flirt in time to

THE VILLA ALBANI.

THE VIEW FROM THE PINCIO.

Offenbach's seductive music. But in the morning hours and at night it is well-nigh deserted; and then the tragic memories, which are forever lurking in the background, advance, and take possession of the height. At such a time the thoughtful visitor should advance to the parapet of the Pincio, and look down on the Piazza del Popolo, from the centre of which rises one of the eleven obelisks brought to Rome from Egypt, memorials of her conquest of the country of the Pharaohs. Situated in full view of the fashionable throng upon the Pincian terraces, this solemn relic of antiquity seems to rebuke the folly of the thoughtless crowd. It would appear old to us if we considered merely the fact that it has been standing in Rome since the commencement of the Christian era; yet its Roman life is but a fraction of its history, for it was hewn from the primitive volcanic granite of the Nile, and had the secrets of past ages graven on

THE PIAZZA DEL POPOLO.

IN THE PINCIAN GARDENS.

its sides a thousand years before the wall of Romulus was
built. It serves to remind us, however, that human nature in
its weaknesses and passions is much the same from age to
age; for this old monolith, which had in Egypt looked on
Cleopatra and her Roman lovers, reared its majestic form
in Rome, when over these Pincian slopes extended, in vo-
luptuous magnificence, the famous Gardens of Lucullus, the
Asiatic sybarite whose luxury exceeded that of kings, and
who, when falsely accused and doomed to die, supped royally
in his villa here; and then, within a perfumed bath, opened
his veins and, not without a certain majesty, took leave of
life. To him succeeded, as the owner of this site, the shameless Messalina who, in her turn, having been condemned
to death, fled through the shadows of her garden, until finally,
nerved to a fate that was inevitable, she pressed a dagger to
her breast, which was then driven home by the soldier sent to
slay her. What wonder that, in the Middle Ages, Nero's rest-

less ghost was thought to wander at night over this hill as a fit place for his crime-haunted spirit? Even in modern times, the Pincio has not been wholly free from desperate deeds, as when the Princess Borghese (sister of Napoleon) saw on its esplanade one of her admirers stab his rival so near to her that the victim's blood crimsoned the panel of her carriage.

Descending from the Pincian Hill, we drove directly to the Roman Forum. I shall never forget the moment when I first beheld it. Emerging from a narrow street I saw before me a sunken square, from which, at various points, rose columns, arches, pedestals, and crumbling walls. The whole scene trembled, for an instant, in my vision, for I knew that one of the greatest desires of my life was on the point of fulfillment, and that I was at last actually gazing on the spot of earth which had been for centuries the brain of the vast Roman Empire, the focus of the power and intelligence of the human race, and frequently the stage on which the most stupendous dramas in Rome's history were performed, with consuls, emperors, and

THE FORUM.

THE TEMPLE OF SATURN.

generals as the actors, and for an audience a dazzled world.

Awed by the memories of the place, I climbed a little elevation and stood beside eight stately columns, — sole relics of the once magnificent Temple of Saturn, erected four hundred and ninety years before the birth of Christ. I looked with reverence upon their scarred, yet polished surfaces. What men whose deeds still influence the world had, like myself, lingered within their shadow! On this, the hand of Scipio may have rested; that, may have felt the touch of Nero or of Catiline. For centuries, this shrine contained the public treasury of Rome; and it was here that Cæsar, marching southward from the Rubicon, and hastening to secure the public funds abandoned by the terrified Senate, encountered the opposing figure of Metellus the Tribune.

THE ARCH OF SEPTIMIUS SEVERUS.

"Stand back, young man," cried Cæsar, "it is easier for me to do a deed than to threaten it!"

As I stood in this historic portico, directly in front of me rose the Arch of Septimius Severus. It is now sadly mutilated; but, seventeen centuries ago, it was adorned with stately columns and statues in relief, while on the summit was a car of victory in bronze, drawn by six horses and containing the statues of Severus and his sons. The structure possessed special interest for me, since, only a few weeks before, I had seen, on the frontier of England and Scotland, the Roman wall, constructed by the Emperor Severus just five years after this gate had been erected in his honor. Summoned from Rome to crush the insurrection

TOURISTS IN THE FORUM.

in the North, he was destined never to pass beneath this arch of victory, but to expire on English soil, near where now the famous York Cathedral rears its noble towers.

While we were standing here, a crowd of tourists suddenly appeared who, as they moved about from place to place, looked, with their opened black umbrellas, like a swarm of mammoth turtles. Paying, apparently, no heed to what their guide was saying, they laughed and talked incessantly. "I wonder," said my friend, "if they appreciate the fact that in this square the

Romans were framing their famous laws while savages were hunting on the site of Paris, and when the Roman legions protested against being led into Britain, urging that it lay beyond the confines of the world!"

Turning from the arch a few steps brought us to the ruins of a circular structure, which formerly marked the centre of old Rome and consequently the centre of the civilized world. It was the site of the famous Golden Milestone, erected by Augustus, from which distances were reckoned to every province of the Em-

THE SITE OF THE GOLDEN MILESTONE.

pire, — Asia Minor, Palestine, Egypt, Greece, Spain, Gaul, and Britain. To all these places had been built, save where the ocean intervened, magnificent roads which were as useful in those days as railways are to us in bringing different lands and cities into swift, sure, and uninterrupted communication. All of these military highways were furnished with milestones and post-houses at regular intervals, and were kept in perfect condition by men who deemed the office of Curator of the public roads a distinguished honor. Cæsar himself was at one time Curator of the Appian Way. Even to-day, the principal roads through England pursue almost the same courses that they did sixteen hundred years ago, and the very stones which form their beds and give them their stability were

COLUMNS OF THE TEMPLE OF VESPASIAN.

laid by Roman hands. Of course the building of these thoroughfares involved enormous difficulties, the chief of which was the conquest of the tribes through whose domains the routes must pass; but how all this laborious unification of the world, and the subjugation of it to one mighty centre, promoted the advance of civilization and specially favored at that time the advent and propagation of Christianity! If Palestine had been an isolated Hebrew country then, the new religion might have perished in its cradle. As it was St. Paul had only to exclaim in Asia Minor, "I appeal to Cæsar," and he was brought to Rome to plead his cause.

A short walk brought us to another portion of the Forum. No graceful columns rose before me here, but there were memories connected with a mass of masonry which I discerned that held me spellbound. For this was the founda-

RUINS OF THE ROSTRA.

tion of the Rostra,— the platform of that Roman eloquence
which even now, when merely followed silently in printed characters, delights the world.   Here Cicero delivered against Antony
the speech that cost the orator his life; and after he had been
put to death, his head and hands were fastened to the Rostra and
exhibited, and Fulvia the wife of the triumvir pierced his tongue
with her bodkin and spat in the dead man's face.   Who could
have dreamed a year before, when Cicero was in his glory, that

JULIUS CÆSAR.

this would be the fate of that
tongue which had so charmed
the people with its silver
speech, and of those hands
whose gestures had lent em-
phasis to the most polished
rhetoric ever framed by man?

What visions of the past
recurred to me while lingering
here! I seemed to see, as if
it were but yesterday, Julius
Cæsar passing through the
Forum on the Ides of March
to the adjacent Senate-House.
The hour for the greatest
tragedy in Roman history
had come.   The shadow of
impending death was hang-

ing over him; but he moved on, unconscious of its presence.
Some one had thrust into his hand the story of the plot and
even the list of the conspirators, but it remained unread.   The
murderers gathered quickly round him, resolved to act immediately, lest their hearts should fail.   Cimber, whom he had
just made Governor of Bithynia, came close, as if to ask a
favor, and dragged his robe from off his shoulders.   Cassius
then stabbed him in the throat.   At this Cæsar sprang to his

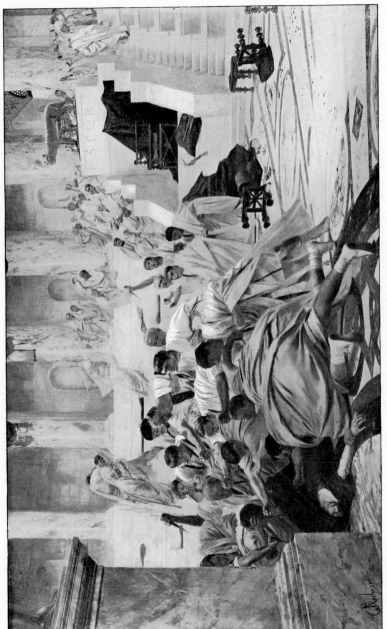

THE MURDER OF CÆSAR.

THE PETITIONERS.

feet and seized the assassin's arm. Meantime, another dagger pierced his breast. He looked around him. What! not one man in all that group to show him gratitude at least for countless favors he had done them? No, nothing but a ring of angry faces, lifted arms and gleaming daggers; a score of cowardly fanatics round one defenseless man. Despite his knowledge of the ingratitude of humanity, one face here drew from Cæsar's lips an exclamation of surprise. "You, too, Brutus?" he exclaimed. That was all; then drawing his mantle over his face, that he might die with dignity, he stood for a moment propped by the blows which he received on every side until,

THE MURDER. (Gérome.)

MARC ANTONY'S ORATION.

as the assassins' arms grew wearied from their cruel work, he sank in death. The Senate rose at once with shrieks and cries and rushed out to the Forum. The murderers waved their gory daggers, and shouted to the populace that Rome was free; but, to their great astonishment, the populace did not respond. An ominous silence filled the city; the climax being reached when, on the Rostra, where he had so often spoken, the body of the murdered chieftain was displayed, wrapped in the mantle he had worn upon the field of victory, now torn with daggers and besmeared with blood. What wonder that under such conditions Marc Antony's superb address roused the populace to madness.

One of the most interesting statues of antiquity now visible at Rome is a colossal figure of Pompey which was discovered, in 1553, buried deep in the soil near the site of the old Senate-House, and exactly under the spot where the historian Suetonius states that it was placed by Augus-

THE STATUE OF POMPEY.

tus. There seems to be no doubt, therefore, that it is the very
statue at the base of which the greatest of all Romans fell;
and, by a strange fatality, perhaps the last glance of the con-

CÆSAR IMPERATOR.

queror of the world,
dimmed by the
swiftly creeping film
of death, rested upon
the statue of his van-
quished rival, which
fixed, unmoved, its
stony gaze upon his
bleeding form. But
did his helpless body,
pierced with ghastly
wounds, prove that
great Cæsar's spirit
was no more? Ah,
no! The jealous and
short-sighted   men
who plunged their
daggers into his
prostrate form had
thought it would be
so; but hardly had
their blows been
given, when to their
great astonishment,
they saw that Cæsar
triumphed over them
in death as he had

done in life. "We have killed the King," said Cicero in bitter dis-
enchantment, "but the kingdom is still with us." And why was it
with them? Because the world had need then of a government
like that of Cæsar's, and it was felt intuitively that Cæsar had

been killed, not for destroying the liberty of the Roman citizen, but because he had suppressed the power of the Aristocracy.

Julius Cæsar is the central figure of antiquity. A skillful lawyer, a brilliant orator, an unsurpassed historian of war, the greatest general of ancient times, a statesman never equaled in stupendous plans, he was the connecting link between a great republic five hundred years old, and the only universal empire the world has ever seen. What wonder that his amiable qualities and glorious genius endeared him to his friends and have enshrined him in the affections of humanity! No foe was ever

more generous than Cæsar. To the captured leaders of the Pompeian party after the battle of Pharsalia, who knelt down in supplication for their lives, Cæsar exclaimed, "Rise! After a victory Cæsar knows no enemies." In the tent of Pompey a secret correspondence was found revealing all the in-

THE ARCH OF TITUS.

trigues of the past few years and implicating, doubtless, some whom the Dictator never had suspected; but Cæsar burned the entire mass unread.

"What are you doing?" inquired Antony in great astonishment. "I am burning these letters," replied Cæsar. "But why?" again demanded Antony. "That I may have," said Cæsar, calmly, "no motive for revenge."

Beyond the Forum extends the Via Sacra, — the fashionable street of ancient Rome. This was to the City of the Cæsars what Broadway now is to New York, or Regent Street to

London.   The poet Ovid, exiled to the Danube, longed for
the splendor of the Sacred Way, as if that were equivalent to
Rome itself, and poured forth his request for a return to it in
unavailing song; while one of Horace's witty satires com-
mences, " I was strolling one day, as is my custom, on the Via
Sacra."

In one place part of the ancient pavement is visible in lava
blocks, which may have been pressed by the sandaled feet of
Cæsar, Cicero, and Virgil.   Especially conspicuous on this
ancient thorough-
fare is the Arch
of Titus which,
even after the
lapse of eighteen
centuries, ranks
among the grand-
est relics of im-
perial Rome, and
is an eloquent re-
minder of the oc-
casions when along
the highway, which
it still adorns, the
splendid Roman

RELIEF IN ARCH.

Triumphs passed with matchless pageantry to reach the
Forum and the Capitol.   Although designed to commemorate
the conquest of Jerusalem by Titus, the sculptured concave of
this arch did not, as was formerly supposed, cast its broad
shadow on the conqueror and his train of captive Jews in the
great celebration of his Triumph, but was erected in his honor
by his brother Domitian shortly after his decease.   There is,
however, no possibility of mistaking its significance; for, on
one side of it, figures, carved in high relief, plainly portray
the Hebrews led in the Triumph of Titus, while on their

shoulders are distinctly visible the seven-branched golden can-
dlestick, the trumpet of the Jubilee, and other treasures from
the Temple of Solomon.   All this is no mere legend, therefore,
to be read in books and dimly understood.   It was an actual
occurrence.   Over this very pavement rolled the chariot of
Titus, drawn by snow-white horses; before him really walked
just such a line of captives from the walls of Zion; while these
hills echoed to the blasts of Roman trumpets, the eagles of
Rome's legions glittered in the sun, and the air throbbed with

the inspiring
shouts of thou-
sands.   What a
suggestive and
realistic teacher,
therefore, of the
Past is this sub-
limely sculptured
portal of old
Rome!

I suppose the
world has never
elsewhere   seen
such a magnifi-

THE CAPTIVE JEWS.

cent pageant as
that presented by a Roman Triumph.   A conqueror expected
and demanded this as a conclusive proof of his success.
To pass along the Via Triumphalis, preceded by the spoils
of conquest and many of the captives he had made was,
naturally, the proudest moment of his life.   Nothing could
have so gratified his personal vanity, or so contributed to
the pride of the Romans who, in beholding such a spectacle,
believed themselves to be, as in truth they were, the masters of
the world.   In a triumphal procession the Senators, who had
decreed the honor to the victorious general, met him at the city

FOUNTAIN IN THE PIAZZA NAVONA.

gates and led the way. After them came the booty of the conquered nation, conveyed either on the shoulders of the slaves and prisoners, or in hundreds of wagons following one after another, in which were placed the pictures, statues, and innumerable ornaments in gold, silver, and bronze. Then were displayed the weapons of the vanquished: shields, battle-axes, swords, and war chariots, together with the crowns and sceptres of defeated kings, the horses, elephants, or dromedaries which

they had ridden, their gorgeous tents and countless proofs of personal luxury. Following them came the most illustrious of the captives: kings, queens, or warriors, as the case might be, usually walk-

THE TRIUMPH OF GERMANICUS.

ing barefooted and accompanied by their families. Sometimes the booty was so large that two entire days were necessary for its exhibition; and, finally, when the minds of the people had been thoroughly impressed with the magnificence and importance of the conquest, the conqueror himself appeared in a triumphal chariot drawn by four or six white horses. Dressed in a purple toga embroidered with gold, and holding a branch of laurel in one hand, and in the other an ivory sceptre, the hero of the Triumph must have seemed the most exalted of his race; and it is not strange that the slave who stood behind him in his car of victory, and held above his head a golden wreath, was bidden to whisper to him ever and anon the words, "Remember thou, too, art a man." Behind them all appeared the representatives of the Roman legions, whose valor and fidelity had won the victory, and who were destined, little by little, to feel their power, until by their decision they made and unmade emperors at will. The ending of these Tri-

A GALLIC CHIEF.

umphs differed greatly according to the character and rank of their participants. The conqueror himself, reaching the Capitol, climbed on his knees the stairway leading to the shrine of Jupiter, and humbly laid the gold wreath on the statue of the deity; the thousands who had brought the spoils along the Via Sacra deposited them within the temple area, and went their way; the soldiers marched back to their camp outside the walls; and in the Forum, the populace was lavishly entertained at the expense of the victorious general, — on one occasion twenty-two thousand

HEAD OF A BARBARIAN.

tables having been spread for such a public banquet. Meantime the principal captive had been cast into the Mamertine
Prison, to meditate, in the appalling darkness of that dungeon,
on the bitterness of life, and to await inevitable death.

What wonder that to avoid such a humiliation the vanquished Cleopatra preferred the poison of the asp!

One object at the terminus of the Sacred Way completely
filled my vision. It was the Colosseum. I wonder if to any

THE COLOSSEUM.

traveler in the world this building has proved disappointing. I
cannot think it possible. All things considered, nothing in
Rome can equal it in grandeur. It is the King of Ruins, desolate but defiant, dethroned and yet sublime. Simple, majestic,
solitary, and unique; tinted by the suns of nearly twenty centuries, it rises at the union of the Sacred and Triumphal Ways,
like the colossal skeleton of Roman power. Before it stands
the almost shapeless mass of the Meta Sudans, the fountain

THE META SUDANS.

where it is sup-
posed the gladia-
tors used to bathe
after the combat,
surrounded, no
doubt, by a gap-
ing crowd, and
petted and ad-
mired by effemi-
nate patricians,
who, with their
soft white hands,
patted the brawny
muscles of the
athletes and of-
fered wagers on
their next encounters. Human nature has not greatly changed
in this respect in eighteen hundred years.

Slowly I made the circuit of the Colosseum, counting the
eighty arches leading to the interior. The eighty-seven thousand people who were often gathered here could find abundant
and substantial
avenues of en-
trance and of
exit. The outer
corridors are
made of mas-
sive blocks of
stone, piled
one upon an-
other and then
bound together
by iron clamps,
as if to last

" ARCHES ON ARCHES."

while Time endured. Thousands of ragged holes in these huge stones show how the highly valued metal was extracted from them in the Middle Ages. There was no danger here of panic or collapse. Woe to the man who trifled with the public in those days! An architect named Atilius tried it once, and built in a provincial town a flimsy amphitheatre which fell, occasioning great loss of life. Tacitus says that fifty thousand people were crushed to death or maimed by this disaster, and then relates the builder's pun-ishment in three short words, which ought to be inscribed above the door of every wretchedly built theatre in the world, " Atilius was banished."

A CORRIDOR.

I had sup-posed that all the pictures I had seen of the in-terior of this mighty edifice would make astonishment impossible ; but nothing had prepared me for the grand reality. The rows of ruined arches, rising in a gigantic circle toward the sky, are overpowering in their im-mensity, and the huge doorways seem like caverns in a moun-tain side, from which wild beasts may even now emerge. To climb to the highest tier, as can be done easily by stairways, and to look thence down a hundred and fifty feet, as into the enor-mous crater of a dead volcano, gives one a sensation obtain-able nowhere else in the whole world.

The walls have now been scraped and cleaned of all the

A GLIMPSE OF THE INTERIOR.

vegetation which had for centuries accumulated on their broken surfaces; but, formerly, wherever wind-blown seeds had found a foothold on these curving slopes, as on a natural hillside, vines twined their arms around the Colosseum's massive columns, as if to hide the memory of its crimes, grasses swayed lightly in the mighty arches, lichens crept timidly along the sides of the arena, and life so far succeeded in replacing death, that botanists were able to compose a large herbarium of plants and flowers growing on these walls. The arena, also, has been largely opened to the day, and one can trace there now, some twenty feet below the arena, the dens for the wild beasts, the openings through which they were fed, the corridors through which they rushed to the arena, and the apartments where the gladiators waited until called to conflict, — probably to death.

To furnish enter-

WAITING FOR THE CONFLICT.

"THUMBS DOWN."

tainment here for the Roman people the entire world was ran-
sacked to secure wild beasts, which it was a crime to kill. Some
nations, conquered by the Romans, had to pay tribute to them
not only in money, but in lions, panthers and tigers, which were
slaughtered in almost incredible numbers. By order of Julius
Cæsar four hundred lions contended at one time, and Caligula
caused five hundred bears to be killed in a single day. Think
what a task it must have been to capture and convey to
Rome, unwounded and alive, these thousands of ferocious
beasts! Before the sports in the arena these animals were
usually kept in dens or cages, and people were allowed to
inspect them. They thus enjoyed the double pleasure of seeing them fight, — first in imagination, then in reality. Bar-
num should have been born eighteen hundred years ago.
With such advantages he would have been the "noblest Roman

of them all." In many conflicts, however, no animals appeared, and only gladiators fought with one another to the death. The well-known painting by Gérome portrays a scene of frequent occurrence in those days. Thousands of men and women, intent upon the combat, are represented glaring with bated breath into the whirl and dust of the arena. The victor pauses in compassion to read the verdict of the populace. The victim also lifts his arm in piteous appeal. Alas! the thumbs of all are turned inexorably downward. It is the fatal signal. The gladiator must die. It seems almost incredible that men should have consented to be butchered thus, merely to make a Roman holiday. Many of them were slaves, or prisoners of war, whose lives were considered of so little value that, while accounts were kept of all

THE PRESERVED WALL.

the expensive elephants and tigers killed, no reckoning seems to have been made of the loss of men! Yet, at least ten thousand athletes were always kept in readiness for the Colosseum, — all of them trained to kill one another, and every one of them certain, sooner or later, to be slain. It has always seemed strange to me that they did not combine more frequently, as Sparticus and his associates did in the days of the Republic, and lose their lives at least, if die they must, in fighting for their liberty.

Since this building was, for nearly four hundred years, the scene not only of gladiatorial combats, but, frequently, of

THE ARENA.

Christian martyrdom, the Church has long regarded it as consecrated ground. Accordingly thirty years ago there stood around the outer edge of the arena, which was carpeted with turf, a line of chapels dedicated to the memory of Christians who had here found death ; while in the centre rose— like an inverted sword, no longer used for bloodshed — the Cross of Christ, emblem of peace and love. I sometimes wish those objects had not been removed, for what could better emphasize the facts of history than the impressive symbol of Christianity, rising above the very place where had so often flowed the blood of its heroic martyrs? Here, too, on

THE MARTYRS.

every Friday afternoon a sermon would be preached, teaching how much the Christian faith once cost, yet how that faith had triumphed over imperial Rome. Does it seem possible that eighty thousand people could be found so bloodthirsty and cruel as to look calmly down upon their fellow-men burning in agony as torches, or torn in pieces by wild beasts?

Can we believe, however, that among those multitudes not one felt pity for the fearless victim who, without weapons, knelt to offer up a prayer, the words of which were lost amid the roar of famished monsters? Were not some responsive hearts impressed and even thrilled by the heroic faith of St. Ignatius who, as the wild beasts leaped into this arena to devour him, exclaimed in a loud voice, " I am as the grain of the field, and must be ground by the teeth of lions, that I may become bread fit for my Master's table "? It was through the influence of Christianity that the gladiatorial combats, finally, came to an end. Four hundred years had rolled

THE MONK'S APPEAL.

away since Christ first taught the brotherhood of man; when, one day, an Oriental monk, Telemachus by name, shocked at these scenes of cruelty and carnage, rushed into the arena, restrained the conqueror's uplifted arm, and begged not only him, but the spectators also, to renounce such deeds forever. Instead of listening, they stoned him to death. Yet he did not die in vain. Christianity had then become the State religion, and so deep and lasting was the influence caused by his protest, that presently the decree went forth that these huge walls should no more echo to the yells of triumph, or to the groans of dying men.

ON THE PALATINE.

Gigantic as the Colosseum is, two-thirds of it has now disappeared. In the fourteenth century it was looked upon as a legitimate quarry from which to extract building materials. Four thousand workmen labored at one time in tearing down its walls. In the year 1452 two thousand five hundred cartloads of it were removed, and furnished material for some of the largest palaces of Rome. "There is no longer any doubt," says the great archæologist, Lanciani, "that the Romans have done more harm to their own city than all invading hosts put together. The action of centuries of natural phenomena, such as hurricanes, earthquakes, fires, and inundations, could not have

A GATEWAY.

accomplished what men have willingly and deliberately done."

Almost in the shadow of the Colosseum stands the Arch of Constantine. It is of unusual interest, not only as the last of the great Roman gates of triumph, but from having been erected only fifteen years before the sovereign whose name it bears transferred the seat of the world's empire from the Tiber to the Bosphorus. One cannot stand before it, therefore, without reflecting sadly that beneath this arch, in the year 330, the Emperor Constantine and his imperial court went forth from Rome forever, and in precisely the opposite direction from that

THE ARCH OF CONSTANTINE.

in which the splendid Triumphs of his predecessors had passed along this same route of the Via Triumphalis and the Via Sacra to the Capitol. It was the expectation of the Emperor, who thus abandoned the Eternal City, that the " New Rome " which he was soon to found beside the Golden Horn, and which now bears his name, would far outshine if not eclipse the City of the Cæsars. But, although Constantinople did become the capital of the Roman Empire, its history was largely one of Oriental intrigue and corruption, till, finally, it passed into the hands of the Sultans. Rome, on the contrary, although deserted by her Emperors, pillaged by barbarians, and left desolate for

WHERE THE TRIUMPHS PASSED.

ages, has never lost her birthright of dominion, and still controls the imagination of more men than when she held the sovereignty of the ancient world; for, by a single coincidence, the very Emperor who left her for another had, by acknowledging the faith of Jesus as the State religion, given her the greatest compensation for her loss. In place of the departing Court arrived the Church, to the authority of Cæsar succeeded the supremacy of Christ, and Rome thenceforth was not alone the sovereign, but the priestess of humanity.

Directly opposite this memorial of Constantine rises the Palatine, the oldest and most aristocratic of Rome's seven hills: oldest, in the sense that it was there, two thousand six hundred years ago, that historic Rome began, with the fortress built by Romulus; and aristocratic, because Plebeians never occupied it. Only Consuls, Emperors, and Patricians dwelt upon the Palatine. A half century ago the hill was covered with old farms and vineyards, and only half-a-dozen unidentified fragments peered above the soil. It was then a place where one could

RUINS ON THE PALATINE.

THE IMPERIAL AMPHITHEATRE.

walk in quiet revery, enjoying thoroughly the classic memories of the locality, without the necessity of studying the ruins
too closely; but now excavations have been made here so exten-
sively that the entire hill resembles a museum of antiquities,
where everything is labeled with a name and number, and
where the visitor becomes exhausted if he attempts to comprehend and recollect the whole. The Palatine is like a golden
book upon whose pages Roman Emperors obliterated and wrote
over one another's records till they have become nearly illegi-
ble. Its leaves have, also, been repeatedly torn and scattered,
till a connected story is almost impossible. I think the best
way, therefore, for the tourist, who does not claim to be an
archæologist, to enjoy the Palatine is to stroll thoughtfully
among its old memorials of imperial luxury, without attempt-
ing to distinguish too minutely their details, and, by accepting
frankly only a general idea of them, to let the impressions of
their magnitude and of the great events which have transpired

here leave on his mind an influence undisturbed by doubts and
acrimonious disputes.

Some portions of the various imperial abodes which have
succeeded one another here have, however, been positively
identified. Thus, we can walk to-day upon a fragment of
the marble pavement of Domitian's banquet-hall; and, looking
round us at its ruined masonry, still lined in places with a
coating of rare marble, can realize how this man — for fifteen
years the ruler of the world — would walk here fearful almost
of his shadow, glancing continually at the surrounding walls,
whose marble surfaces were polished like a mirror, to see that
no assassin followed him. Yet his precautions were in vain,
and his apprehensions only too well founded. Here the freed-
man Stephanus (probably instigated by the Empress herself
who, with her courtiers, trembled for her life), struck down at
last the hated tyrant and gave the weary world relief.

Another portion of these ruins about which there can be
no doubt is the *crypto portico*, or subterranean gallery, through

EXCAVATIONS ON THE PALATINE.

which the Emperors could enter or leave the palace unobserved.
It was in this passageway that the youthful monster of iniquity
and cruelty, Caligula, was murdered; and we may look now on
the very walls that echoed to his shrieks and cries for mercy.
What a change had taken place in the bright boy, whose
advent to the throne only four years before had been so warmly
welcomed, on the death of Tiberius! A descendant of the
beloved Augustus, and a son of the admired Germanicus, he

was expected to prove an ideal ruler. So young and popular
was he, that though his name was Caius, every one called him
by the pet name given him when a child, from the *caligæ*, or
soldiers' boots, which it was his delight as a boy to wear; and
as Caligula, indeed, the world has known him for nearly nineteen hundred years. The only possible explanation of the
horrors of his reign seems to be that for the last three years
of his life his mind was unbalanced. If his insanity had

CALIGULA'S BRIDGE.

merely shown itself in harmless eccentricities, like calling himself divine, and conferring on his favorite horse the title of Consul, and feeding it with gilded corn, and wine in golden bowls, he would not have been dangerous; but a tigerish thirst for blood seemed to be ever on the point of completely mastering Caligula, and Cruelty soon chose him for her favorite pupil. Thus, one day at a public banquet when the Consuls were reclining with him at table, this mad Emperor suddenly burst into roars of laughter, and to their natural inquiry as to the cause of his mirth, he replied that he was thinking how, by a word, he could cause their heads to roll upon the floor. One day, too, when fondling his wife's neck, he is said to have remarked to her, "Beautiful as it is, how easily I could cut your head from it!" When we consider all the crimes committed on the Palatine by these imperial monsters, maddened by unbounded power,

PAVEMENT OF THE PALACE.

and realize that we walk through the very rooms where, for example, Nero murdered his half-brother Britannicus, and where
Emperor Claudius ate the poisoned mushrooms, prepared for
him by his wife in order to elevate her son Nero to the throne,
and where half a score of the imperial family were assassinated, Rome's vices seem to eclipse her virtues, and the imposing arches and huge walls — which have arisen, ghost-like, from
their shrouds of centuries — seem haunted by appalling memories, as if the residents of the Palatine had been fiends in

PROCESS OF EXCAVATION.

human form.
Yet, such
wise and vir-
tuous rulers
as Augustus,
Nerva, Tra-
jan, Hadrian,
and Marcus
Aurelius al-
most atone
for the hide-
ous monsters
whodisgraced
humanity as
Roman Em-
perors; and
the incalculable debt we owe to Rome should never be lost sight
of in our horror of the vices and atrocities of her evil sovereigns.

The Romans as a people are immortalized in history as the
Titanic race which conquered, civilized, and held for centuries
the whole known world from the Pillars of Hercules to the
Euphrates, and from the moors of Scotland to the cataracts of
the Nile. Moreover, such was the magnificent system of
government founded by them with their marvelous genius for
practical administration, that even under the worst emperors

AUGUSTUS.

justice and order were, as a rule, enforced throughout the entire Empire. Aside from certain cruel acts originating in the tyrant's mind, the world at large was never better governed than by Tiberius, when he was living in seclusion on the island of Capri. Deified despots on the Palatine might kill or torture hundreds, but the unnoticed millions lived, loved, labored, and lay down to die in peace.

One afternoon, to vary our experiences in this wondrous city, we drove beyond its walls into the beautiful gardens of the Villa Borghese, which, like so many other lovely parks in the vicinity of Rome (now rapidly diminishing, alas, through the greed of speculative builders), attract the visitor to their shaded avenues, when wearied for a time with ruins, galleries, and churches. The air here is invariably fragrant with the breath of flowers, and during the delicious days of spring the velvet sward

TIBERIUS.

is carpeted with countless violets and anemones, that flush
the withered cheek of Rome and make it glow again with
youthful beauty. Nor are these gardens wanting in agreeable
memories. For centuries they have been the favorite haunt of
artists, and under not a few of these immemorial pines Raphael
used to walk at sunrise, enamored of some fair ideal, which,
later in the day, would find expression on his canvas.

On entering the villa itself, I looked around me with astonishment. This surely was a palace rather than a villa. The

IN THE VILLA BORGHESE.

ceilings glowed
with brilliant
frescos; the walls
were encased in
many-colored
marbles and cov-
ered with forms
and tableaux in
relief; while on
the beautiful
mosaic pavement
stood rare vases,
inlaid tables, and
pedestals sup-
porting many
busts and statues,
modern and an-
tique. Its ancient treasures are especially remarkable, not
only in themselves, but on account of their peculiar origin.
After his marriage with Pauline Bonaparte, sister of Napoleon, the Prince Borghese, owner of the villa, was requested
by his imperial brother-in-law to sell him some of his statues to increase the treasures of the Louvre at Paris. The
Prince complied, but was immediately inconsolable at having
done so. Finally, half in hope, half in despair, he had his vast

THE FOUNTAIN OF TREVI.

estates once more dug over and explored, with the result that
from the wondrous soil of old Italy was brought to light a second collection of marbles, equal, if not superior, to the first.
Think, then, what marvels of artistic skill may still repose
within the dust of Rome, from which, without even leaving his
own property, a Prince could thus extract a gallery of statues!

Nothing gives us a better idea of the magnificence of
ancient Rome than the astounding wealth which its soil is still
capable of yield-
ing. Thus, merely
in the brief inter-
val of fifteen
years, — between
1873 and 1888, —
there were un-
earthed, in laying
the foundations
for new buildings
in Rome, one hun-
dred and ninety-
two marble stat-
ues, several of
which were mas-
terpieces ; two

RARE WORKS OF ART.

hundred and sixty-six busts, seventy-seven columns, twenty-
four hundred lamps, three hundred and sixty cameos, four
hundred and five bronzes, and thirty-seven thousand gold and
silver coins.

No city in the world was ever more abundantly supplied
with water than the City of the Cæsars, and of the numerous
springs which poured the precious liquid into Rome one of the
purest and most copious is now known as the Fountain of
Trevi. Marcus Agrippa brought its silvery current to the city,
a score of years before the birth of Christ, through one of the

gigantic aqueducts that, with their massive arches, formed elevated pathways for the mountain streams which flowed toward
Rome and entered it as railroads now converge from different
points to one of our modern cities. It was then called the
"Fountain of the Virgin," because its source had been made
known to Marcus Agrippa's thirsty soldiers by a youthful
maiden. In the great flood of barbarism that swept over Rome
in the fifth century, this aqueduct was broken, and its flow of
water ceased for a thousand years ; but, in 1560, Pope Pius IV.
caused the colossal conduit to be repaired, and brought the
water once more into the city. In 1735 its terminus was
marked by an enormous structure, which, although more remarkable than beautiful, is still sufficiently imposing to leave
upon the memory a deep impression. The architectural back-

THE FOUNTAIN PAOLINO.

ground for
the running
water re-
sembles the
façade of a
huge palace,
and is adorned
with lofty col-
umns and stat-
ues, and two
reliefs, one of
which repre-
sents the tra-
ditional maid-
en pointing out
the spring to
the Roman
soldiers, while
the other por-
trays Agrippa

studying a plan
for the construc-
tion of the aque-
duct. At the base
a mass of rocks
and masonry has
been arranged,
like boulders piled
up by an ava-
lanche, among
which Neptune's
ocean chariot,
drawn by two sea
monsters, seems
to be stranded,
despite the stren-

AN AËRIAL WATERWAY.

uous efforts of a score of Tritons to release it. Meanwhile,
around the ocean deity, a flood of water bursts forth
through a hundred apertures, and after sporting madly
with old Neptune's horses and attendants, and mockingly
eluding them by leaping over barriers, darting under rocks
and wriggling through a thousand crevices, at last falls
breathless into a marble reservoir, and lies demurely in the
sunshine, offering no resistance to the men and women who
come to fill their jars and pitchers from its overflow. This
fountain well repays a visit by moonlight, for the proportions
of the structure and the forms of the statues then seem infinitely more majestic than by day; while, in the hush of evening, the innumerable little streams, which interlace the rocks
like silver threads, seem to be murmuring of the dripping ferns
and mosses in their far-off mountain home. Who has not
sometimes pitied such imprisoned water, which cannot take the
course that it would naturally choose, but is compelled to flow
along a route determined by the will of man?

It is estimated that, during the period of the Empire, Rome's supply of water amounted to three hundred and thirty-three million gallons daily; and to-day, thanks to her ancient rulers, she is better supplied with water than any other capital in the world. Four different aqueducts bring to it, even now, an amount equal to one hundred and ten gallons daily *per capita*, while London furnishes its inhabitants with only thirty gallons each, and Paris seventy. It is not strange, therefore, that, with this magnificent volume pouring into it continually, Rome has been called a city of fountains. There are, in fact, in the City of the Tiber, twenty-eight fountains in the different squares, and more than three hundred public conduits that flow, night and day, into huge stone watering troughs.

THE APPIAN WAY, AND AQUEDUCTS.

The Capitol, like all the others of Róme's seven hills, is eloquent of history. It was the scene of many of Rome's earliest glories and her latest crimes. Above the city, on one side of it, was the Tarpeian Rock, down which all traitors and the basest criminals were hurled to death; and on its temple-crowned plateau all the distinguished Romans of antiquity have often stood. Here Brutus, too, harangued the populace after the murder of Cæsar; and it was on the steps which the present modern stairway has now replaced, that Rienzi (" Last of the

RUINS OF THE CLAUDIAN AQUEDUCT.

Roman Trib-
unes") fell, bleed-
ing from twenty
wounds, while
from a window
in their palace
his beautiful
young wife looked
out and saw his
tragic death.

Bearing these
facts in mind, I
climbed the noble
staircase leading
to the summit,
and stood within

THE CAPITOL.

the Square of the Capitol. The bronze statue of Marcus
Aurelius in the centre of the area is especially interesting

THE SQUARE OF THE CAPITOL.

because it is the
only equestrian
figure which has
come down to
us of all that
once adorned
imperial Rome;
and what a
comment on the
character of the
Middle Ages is
the fact that it
owed its preser-
vation to mis-
taken identity!
For it was then

THE STATUE OF MARCUS AURELIUS.

supposed to be a representation of Constantine, whose statue, since he had been a Christian Emperor, was spared while those of Pagan sovereigns were, as far as possible, destroyed. Critics have usually been unfriendly to this work of art, but the horse, at least, was greatly admired by Michelangelo, who upon one occasion clapped his hands together as he looked at it, exclaiming enthusiastically, *"Cammina!"* — Get up! — as though that word would start it into motion.

No reader of the "Marble Faun" will forget Hawthorne's description of a visit made by moonlight to this statue, which he calls the most majestic representation of the kingly character that the world

THE HALL OF THE EMPERORS.

has ever seen. Certain it is, that as I looked upon this figure of Rome's noblest sovereign, and realized how it once had stood thus in the Forum, when the whole world lay subject to that outstretched hand, I felt that I had been brought nearer to the past, than even by the Arch of Titus, or the Colosseum.

Leaving the square, I entered the Museum of the Capitol, and found myself in the apartment known as the Hall of the Emperors. This had for me a novel interest. Hitherto I had been treading in the footsteps of the ancient Romans, but here I met them face to face. Around the walls, I saw in a long double line statues and busts of Roman Emperors and their families, all of which are authentic likenesses, cut in the marble

CLASSIC BUSTS.

seventeen or eighteen hundred years ago, and placed side by side for close inspection and comparison. Beginning at random, I wrote in my note-book the names of these imperial characters and their modes of death. After a time I paused and observed the record. It was as follows: Julius Cæsar, murdered; Agrippina (represented in the seated statue), died of enforced starvation; Caligula, her son, assassinated; Claudius, poisoned; Messalina, his wife, put to death by order of her husband; Agrippina, mother of Nero, murdered by her son; Nero himself, died by suicide; Poppæa, his wife, kicked to death by Nero; the Emperor Galba, murdered; Otho, died by suicide;

Titus, supposed to have been poisoned; Domitian, murdered; Lucilla, daughter of Marcus
Aurelius, put to death at Capri; Commodus
and his wife, both murdered; Pertinax,
assassinated; Julianus, stabbed to death;
and, finally, Caracalla, Geta his brother,
and Macrinus his successor, all murdered;
Elagabalus, Alexander Severus, Maximinus,
and Maximus Tyrannus, all killed; besides
twelve others, all of whom died a violent death!
A more appalling commentary on the vices of
the Roman Empire it would be hard to find

VITELLIUS.

than that afforded by this portrait-gallery of its rulers.

Halting before a gross and sensual face, I read beneath it
the name "Vitellius," and knew that I was looking on the portrait of the most disgusting of the wearers of the purple. How
swinish must his actual appearance have been if this, his bust,
which was no doubt made as flattering as possible, depicts him
as a drunken glutton! Small wonder is it that he reigned but
a few months, and that when the opposing party found him on
the Palatine, stupefied by debauchery, short work was made
of his assassination, and that after his head had been carried
joyfully through the streets of Rome, the body was thrown into
the Tiber. It is appropriate, therefore, that this hill, so
haunted with suggestive, melancholy memories, should
have inspired the historian Gibbon, as he sat one
evening amid its ruins, to write the "Decline and
Fall of the Roman Em-
pire."

On the following
day, I left the city by
the St. Paul gate and
drove beyond the Ro-
man walls along the

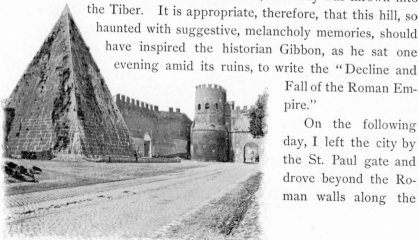

THE ST. PAUL GATE.

A HALL IN THE PALAZZO COLONNA.

ancient road which formerly led to Rome's great harbor, Ostia, at the terminus of the Tiber. A sharply pointed pyramid of marble, one hundred and fourteen feet in height, attracted my attention, not only as a work of art, but as a proof that the pyramidal form is best adapted to resist the ravages of Time; for, though surrounded by the wrecks of centuries, this structure is still perfectly preserved, and since St. Paul was led along this road to martyrdom, it no doubt looked to him almost exactly as it appears to-day. It is older than Christianity, having been erected here, as a grand funeral monument to Caius Cestius, a generation before the Christian era.

We drove along the ancient thoroughfare until we reached the noble church erected to the memory of the great Apostle, and called "St. Paul's without the walls." I paused in admiration on the thresh-old. Before me stretched away in dazzling perspec-tive a glorious nave, four hun-dred feet in length, surmount-ed by a roof of gold, and paved

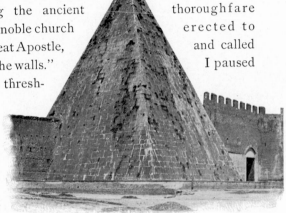

THE PYRAMID OF CESTIUS.

with blocks of variegated marble, which glittered like the surface of a sunlit lake. To right and left, like stately trees, from out this beautiful expanse arose a multitude of granite columns, each of which was a single block of stone, polished as smooth as glass, and crowned with an elaborate capital. Above these was a row of circular mosaic portraits of the Popes, apparently gazing down with pride upon the splendid scene. The reverence felt by Christians for this church is principally due, however, not to its lavish ornamentation or even to its

"ST. PAUL'S WITHOUT THE WALLS."

great antiquity, but to the fact that under the High Altar, of jasper, malachite, and alabaster, is a sarcophagus which, according to the traditions of the Church from earliest times, contains the body of St. Paul.

"How is it possible," I asked of my companion, "that this grand edifice can be so old, and yet so marvelously fresh and beautiful?"

"In one sense it is modern," was the answer; "the ancient church was terribly injured by a conflagration seventy years ago, and much that you admire has been placed here since that time. It is true, the mighty arch above the altar is a part of the original

A SIDE AISLE IN ST. PAUL'S.

church, erected here in the fourth century after Christ; but
you would never guess how recent is the origin of the four
columns which support the altar canopy. They are of tinted
alabaster, and were presented to the Pope by Mehemet Ali,
the bloodthirsty Khedive of Egypt, and a devotee of Islam."

Leaving this noble sanctuary, a short drive brought us to
the most interesting historic thoroughfare in the world, the

THE VIA APPIA.

Appian Way. As we have seen, the Romans were the road-
builders of antiquity, and this military highway to the south
was admirably constructed more than three hundred years before the birth of Christ. It is an impressive hour that one
spends in driving on this "Queen of Roads," as it was fondly
called. The desolate Campagna, on the right and left, was
once so thickly strewn with towns and villages that it was difficult to tell just where the city ended and its environs began.
To-day, beneath its undulating shroud of turf, which faithful

Nature every springtime strews with flowers, there seems to lie
a buried world; while, here and there, like scattered companies
in an irregular procession of prehistoric giants, the fragments
of Rome's mighty aqueducts stride across the lonely plain.

For miles, on both sides of the Appian Way, are the ves-
tiges of ruined sepulchres, no less than thirty thousand of which
have been counted. Once they were beautiful specimens of
Roman art, encased in marble and adorned with statues; but
all that ornamentation has long since been stolen from the
dead, to decorate the structures of the living. It seems to us
extremely inappropriate that this busy thoroughfare should have
been the fashionable burial-place of ancient Rome; but the
Romans were not fond of quiet cemeteries. They wished their
bodies to be laid away near some great artery of human life,
where their elaborate monuments might recall them to their
passing friends, and, possibly, remind them to enjoy life while it

TOMB OF CÆCILIA METELLA.

still was theirs.
That some of
these funeral
monuments were
imposing as well
as elegant in ap-
pearance, is proved
by the well-known
tomb of Cæcilia
Metella, that

. . . "stern round
tower of other days
Firm as a fortress
with its fence of
stone."

Though it has
greatly suffered

RUINED SEPULCHRES.

at the hands of Rome's despoilers, its ponderous form still
grandly dominates the road of Appius Claudius and hints to us
of what its former appearance must have been, when its huge
circular mass, no less than two hundred and ten feet in circumference, was sheathed with marble which, like the ornaments of
all the other tombs along this highway, has been stripped off
to be converted into lime or to adorn modern structures.

Byron's immortal lines upon this "woman's grave" are too
well known to be cited here, but they exemplify the priceless
debt which tourists in Italy owe the author of " Childe Harold "
for the incomparable stanzas devoted to descriptions of this land
of art and history. In Rome, especially, our greatest pleasure
does not come to us from what we know, but from what we
feel; and no other writer has interpreted the exalted sentiments
of admiration, wonder, sympathy, and sadness inspired by the
" Mother of dead empires " as has Byron, who imparts to every
object the indubitable touch of genius.

THE GRAVES OF KEATS AND HIS FRIEND SEVERN.

There is almost no limit to the historic memories awakened by this ancient highway. Along this route, for example, came the imposing funeral procession of the Emperor Augustus, bringing his body back to Rome for burial; by this road, also, was conveyed to figure in a Roman triumph the beautiful captive, Zenobia, Queen of Palmyra; along this highway, as he went to Baiæ on the Bay of Naples, Nero was followed by a retinue of one thousand wagons, and his wife Poppæa by a train of five hundred she-asses, that she might enjoy a bath in their milk every day; and it was from the Appian Way that St. Paul gained his first view of the Eternal City, as he advanced to preach there a religion which was to make of Rome the central city of Christianity.

Behind the marble pyramid which for two thousand years has held the dust of Caius Cestius, lies the beautiful Protestant Cemetery, dear to all English-speaking visitors because of the illustrious dead who slumber in its sacred precincts. What traveler has not breathed a sigh in standing here beside the violets and daisies which, even in winter, grow above the grave of the poet Keats, who died in Rome at the age of twenty-five, the victim of malignant criticism which his sensitive nature could not bear? Who unmoved can read upon his tombstone

the words which he requested should be there inscribed, "Here
lies one whose name was writ in water"? Poor Keats! he is
admired and honored now. Why is it that in so many instances
it is only Death that clears our vision, and makes us generous
and just?

It is appropriate that the poet Shelley, also, should be
buried here, for of this cemetery he had written, "It might
make one in love with death to think that one should be
buried in so sweet a place." In fact, less than a year had
elapsed after the death of Keats, when Shelley's heart (the
only portion of his body unconsumed upon the funeral pyre)
was brought hither by Lord Byron for its final resting-place.
Upon the tombstone, therefore, are inscribed the words, "*Cor
Cordium*" — A heart of hearts. I cannot think of any spot on
earth more suitable for a poet's grave than this; not only from
its natural beauty, but from the fact that when a flood of sunset
glory turns these paths to gold, and one looks upward from
them to Rome's seven hills, the solemn and unrivaled memories

of the place
suggest re-
pose and
peace, and
sad, poetic
dreams of
days that are
no more.

A little
distant from
the Appian
Way are the
enormous
ruins of the
Baths of Car-
acalla. There

SHELLEY'S GRAVE.

is nothing now in the world that corresponds to the magnificent
establishments of ancient Rome which her Emperors founded to
contribute to the cleanliness, pleasures, and luxuries of the people.
They were not merely baths on a lavish and prodigious scale, but,
also, formed the meeting places of literary men, where lectures
were delivered, poems read, and philosophical themes debated.
Athletes gave exhibitions there of skill and strength.   Musicians

THE BATHS OF CARACALLA.

showed their talents, and every form of physical improvement
was competently taught and sedulously cultivated in their various halls.   It has been calculated that sixty-two thousand people could have bathed at any hour in the public baths of Rome,
not to mention the smaller establishments in private houses.
Some of the noblest works of art which had been brought
to Rome from Greece and other conquered countries were
placed in these resorts.   One statue, by Lysippus, which now
stands in the Vatican and represents an athlete scraping the

oil from his arm, was such a favorite with the public that when Tiberius removed it to his palace, popular indignation compelled him to return it to its former position in the Baths of Agrippa. Whatever may be said of the moral delinquencies of the old Romans, they certainly were physically clean. The Emperor Commodus used to bathe eight times a day, and even took his meals in a bath.

THE ATHLETE SCRAPING HIMSELF.

It was customary for wealthy Romans to bathe at least twice a day, the baths being followed by sprinkling with perfumed water, anointing with fine lubricant oil, and massage. An enormous number of slaves were always in attendance at the Roman baths, thoroughly skilled in administering to the physical requirements of the bathers. Among them were tailors who cleaned and pressed clothes, barbers, masseurs, shampooers, anointers, chiropodists, manicures, and men who extracted superfluous hairs.

The Baths of Caracalla were enclosed by porticos nearly a mile in length, where those who had bathed could take gentle exercise while conversing with their friends. Within the limits of this establishment were, also, luxuriant gardens and a courtyard for gymnastic

RUINS OF ROMAN BATHS.

exercises.   Here, too, was a reservoir surrounded by sixteen hundred seats of sculptured marble, and in its largest pool three thousand people could bathe at one time.   The ruins of the Baths of Caracalla are now carefully preserved under the supervision of the Government; but, alas! both time and man have injured them so greatly that it is difficult to form more than a vague idea of what their stupendous arches and enormous areas signify.   We know, however, that

A CORNER IN THE IMPERIAL BATHS.

they contained a theatre, a museum, a library, and halls for conversation, study, and oratory, all of them decorated with the choicest works of art, fine marble, and beautiful mosaics.   It is not strange, therefore, that the Romans who had leisure for such occupations passed many hours every day at the baths.   They were the most luxurious of clubs, where, in addition to every personal attention, could be enjoyed the society of friends, together with amusements, concerts, recitations, and gymnastic exercises.   Excavations have, also, revealed the fact that beneath this vast establishment were subterranean passages with frequent entrances to the main floor above, so that the servants of the place could go from one part of the building to another without crossing the rooms and mingling with the assembled crowds of patricians.

Most travelers, in their eagerness to reach St. Peter's, forget that on the way to it are some important relics of imperial

HADRIAN'S TOMB.

Rome.   One is the bridge of San Angelo, erected seventeen hundred years ago by Hadrian, as a grand avenue of approach to the stupendous mausoleum which he built to contain his own remains and those of his successors.

From what is left of it, to-day, we can form little idea of the original magnificence of this imperial tomb; yet it is certain that its circular tower, one thousand feet in circumference, was formerly covered with Parian marble, and adorned with fine Greek statues and columns of variegated marble and porphyry. Upon the summit, also, stood a colossal figure of its founder, only the head of which has been preserved. Poor Hadrian! He little thought that all the splendid ornaments upon his sepulchre would,

THE BRIDGE OF SAN ANGELO.

a few centuries after his death, be pried off and hurled down upon an army of barbarians who, nevertheless, having gained possession of the Eternal City, would sack this burial-place of Roman Emperors, and, seizing its alabaster urns, give to the winds the dust of Marcus Aurelius, Antoninus Pius, Caracalla, Commodus, Septimus Severus, and Hadrian himself.   In the seventeenth century many statues were found in the moat surrounding this mausoleum, among them being the colossal Head of Hadrian, now in the Vatican, the Dancing Faun of the Uffizi Gallery in Florence, and the Barberini Faun in Munich, all of which, with many others, had been lying there for at least one thousand two hundred years.

"Look toward the summit of the structure," said my friend, "while I remind you of another change that has here taken place."

I did so, and beheld a huge bronze statue of the Archangel Michael sheathing his sword.

"In the sixth century after Christ," continued my companion, "a plague was devastating Rome. One day Pope Gregory the Great was leading a procession across this bridge to pray to Heaven for relief, when he beheld above the tomb of Hadrian a vision of the Archangel replacing his sword in its scabbard, as if the work of destruction were concluded. The plague, in fact, at once abated, and the statue stands here to commemorate the event. Moreover, it has given a new name to this imperial sepulchre, for now its usual title is the 'Castle of the Holy Angel.'"

Leaving this famous edifice, a few steps brought us to the square which forms the approach to St. Peter's. Despite the many visits I have since made to it, I can recall with perfect vividness my first impressions. The grandeur of the intervening space, the curving colonnades on either side, the lofty obelisk, the breadth of the gigantic edifice,

THE ARCHANGEL.

THE SQUARE OF ST. PETER'S.

all these were even more than I had dared anticipate; yet when
I looked up toward the mighty dome, which I had thus far seen
only at a distance, I felt a pang of disappointment. The dome
seemed low to me, and being concealed by the unfortunate façade, actually diminished as I advanced across the area. That
this impression is produced is not, however, the fault of Michelangelo. His plan was to construct the church in the form
of a Greek cross, with equal arms, having in front a portico
which would have left the whole dome visible from the square;
but, after his death, the design was changed to that of a Latin
cross, and the façade was placed three times as far in front of
the dome as the great Florentine had intended, so that on near
approach much of the cupola's majesty is lost.

The Egyptian obelisk, which occupies the centre of the
Piazza, is a solid block of reddish granite, the gilded cross of
which glitters one hundred and thirty-two feet above the pavement. A Pagan obelisk appears at first an inappropriate deco-

A FOUNTAIN IN THE SQUARE.

ration for a Christian church; but when this shaft was brought from Egypt eighteen hundred years ago, it was placed in the Circus of Nero, where many Christians suffered martyrdom. When, therefore, this magnificent basilica was built, so near the site of the Neronian circus that a part of the church's southern wall rests on the ruins of the ancient seats for the spectators, what could be more appropriate than that this ancient monolith, which had looked down upon so many scenes of suffering, should be erected here to hold up, as it were, exultingly, the Cross of Christ, which had at last so permanently and completely triumphed over the sword of Rome?

The porticos on either side of St. Peter's Square are gigantic. No temple in the world can boast of corridors of approach to equal them. Each has four rows of columns, forty-eight feet high; the space beneath their curving roofs is fifty-five feet wide; through either of

ONE OF THE PORTICOS.

AMONG THE COLUMNS.

them, were the central shafts removed, could be driven a car of victory drawn by six horses harnessed abreast; and, as if this were not enough, along their parapets are two hundred and thirty-six statues, each ten feet in height. So well adapted are these curving colonnades to the grand edifice to which they lead, that they suggest a mother's outstretched arms.

Ascending the long flight of broad low steps, I pushed aside the quilted leathern curtain at the entrance and stood within St. Peter's. No illustration or description can do justice to the vast interior, yet I can never forget my first bewildering glimpse

of that unrivaled edifice. One hundred and fifty feet above me curved a glorious arch of sunken coffers dazzling with inlaid gold. Beneath this I looked on and on through a dusky splendor, hazy with incense, till I with

THE FIRST VIEW OF THE INTERIOR.

difficulty saw the gilded shrines a tenth of a mile away. It made me think of a vast mountain cavern lined with precious stones. To right and left rose huge rectangular columns, coated with precious marbles; while through the lofty arches, spanning the broad space between them, I could discern a number of imposing chapels, lavishly adorned.

It requires time to comprehend the immensity of St. Peter's, and it is usually only after several visits that one is able to appreciate its enormous size. It is so vast that we inevitably lose at first our sense of true proportion, and our bewildered minds must readapt themselves, and grow to their new and strange environment. Thus, people in the distance, who appear to us like

THE BAPTISMAL FONT.

pygmies, are really men and women of the usual height. The bases of the columns which seem low to us, we find to be on a level with our heads. The spaces in the huge pilasters look like slender flutings, but are in reality niches deep enough to hold colossal statues. Perhaps we think that the font of holy water in St. Peter's is no larger than those in ordinary churches; but when we examine it more closely, we discover that the marble cherubs supporting it, which at a distance look like children, are fully equal in dimensions to adults.

THE OLD CEREMONY OF PAPAL BENEDICTION.

A MOSAIC PICTURE.

There are many similar illusions in St. Peter's. Thus, its mosaic copies of famous paintings look exactly as if painted upon canvas, but are in truth composed of thousands of pieces of variously tinted stone, which reproduce to perfection every shade of color and even every expression of the original. The delicacy of this work and the length of time required for one picture (sometimes twenty years) render these copies of enormous value; yet there are nearly one hundred of them here, preserving, as it were, imperishably, the masterpieces of Raphael, Guido Reni, Domenichino, and many others whose genius has enriched Christianity.

On entering the side aisles of St. Peter's, their height, the grand Corinthian columns which adorn

A SIDE AISLE.

THE TOMB OF CLEMENT XIII.

each altar, and the sculptured monuments at every turn astonished and bewildered me. Each of these corridors is a kind of Papal Appian Way, since they are lined with splendid tombs commemorating those who have been privileged to occupy St. Peter's chair, one hundred and thirty-two of whom have been buried here. One of the finest of these mausoleums is that of Pope Clement XIII. by Canova. Over the lion-guarded entrance to the crypt is a statue of the Pontiff kneeling in prayer; while on one side of the portal stands the figure of Religion, holding the Cross, and on the other reclines the Genius of Death with inverted torch. The latter is by far the most beautiful statue in St. Peter's, and ranks as one of the

THE GENIUS OF DEATH.

finest productions of Canova's genius.   By many it is thought
to be his masterpiece.   At all events, it was the work which gave
him greatest fame, and placed him in the foremost rank of
European sculptors.   When it was first exposed to the view of
the public, Canova, disguised as an abbé, mingled with the
spectators and listened to their comments.   In doing so he must
have been convinced how much easier it is to criticise than
to create.   They could pass judgment on it in a moment; but
he had labored upon it
for eight years.

Above the grand High
Altar, just beneath the
centre of the dome, is a
magnificent canopy of
gilded bronze.   In any
other sanctuary in the
world it would appear
colossal, but amid these
surroundings its actual
magnitude escapes us.   It
is, however, nearly one
hundred feet in height,
and the cost of gilding it
is said to have been a
hundred thousand dollars.

THE HIGH ALTAR.

Before it is a curving balustrade of marble, on which are burning
eighty-nine golden lamps, the light of which is never suffered to
expire.   It is evident, then, that this is an altar of unusual sanc-
tity; and, in fact, none but the Pope may here officiate, or, possibly, a Cardinal especially appointed for that honor.   What,
therefore, is the treasure guarded here so jealously?   What is the
precious relic which these walls enclose, and over which the huge
dome rises like a miniature sky?   It is the grave of the Gali-
lean fisherman whose name the temple bears.   Advancing to

the balustrade, I looked down into the crypt, and perceived the entrance to the tomb. The air was heavy with incense, a row of golden lamps cast a faint lustre on the shimmering marble and the sacred shrine; hundreds of feet above, the dome of Michelangelo seemed the gigantic shell, of which this sepulchre of St. Peter was the pearl; and, over us — so far away that the unaided vision could scarcely read them — there glittered in mosaic letters, six feet long, the words addressed so many years

THE TOMB OF ST. PETER.

ago to a poor peasant of Judea: "Thou art Peter; and on this rock I will build my church."

Never shall I forget the moment, when, turning my gaze heavenward, I gained a view of the interior of the stupendous dome, all radiant with golden mosaics. To look up into this from below affected me as it does to gaze into a profound abyss; and when, having climbed a winding staircase, I stepped out upon a balcony within the dome, I clutched the railing for a moment, feeling as if the earth had suddenly dropped away and left me up among the clouds. Here, more than anywhere else, one thinks with admiration of the genius which could raise a dome like this toward heaven. For, between the worshiper on the pavement and the summit is a space of four hundred and forty feet; and three ordinary churches, spires and all,

STATUE OF ST. PETER.

could be placed
side by side be-
neath this mighty
canopy without
encroaching on
the body of the
church, with two
hundred feet to
spare between the
tops of the spires
and the keystone
of the arch.

St. Peter's
may be appropri-
ately likened to a

A SECTION OF THE DOME.

city, rather than to a sanctuary, whose streets are marble and
whose sky is gold; for, beneath its ceilings, covered with gilded
ornamentation in relief, are no less than forty-four altars, seven
hundred and forty-eight columns, and a population of three

A BIT OF THE CEILING.

hundred and
ninety statues.
Aside from its ec-
clesiastics there
is, also, a colony
of workmen
called San Pie-
trini, who live in
houses on its
roof and, to a cer-
tain extent, are
governed by laws
and customs of
their own. It is
a cosmopolitan

city, at all events, for in these aisles are placed confessionals for every prominent language of Christendom, so that a Roman Catholic from any land may here confess his sins and receive absolution.

Emerging, finally, from St. Peter's we stood once more within its spacious square, and looked no longer toward the church, but toward the lofty building towering far above the colonnades. I gazed upon it with the keenest interest; for to whatever faith the traveler belongs, he cannot fail to recollect that this is deemed by millions of his race the central structure of Christianity, since it is the residence of the Pope, — the Vatican. Through the kindness of the American Catholic College in Rome, many visitors from this country, whether they are Protestants or Catholics, may be presented to the Pope. I cannot speak too highly of the courtesy extended by this institution, not only thus but in a multitude of ways, to travelers of every creed.

In company with two of its officers, on my first visit to

THE VATICAN.

A GALLERY IN THE VATICAN.

Rome, I found myself one day in a long corridor of the Vatican, awaiting a presentation to Pope Pius IX. While lingering there in expectation of his coming, we talked together in low tones of the man we were about to see, remembering that many years before, there came to Pius VII. an officer of his guard who begged to tell him the great sorrow of his life, — that he was subject to attacks of epilepsy. Existence, therefore, was so terrible that he was tempted to destroy himself. The Holy Father gave him excellent advice, told him to implore God for relief, and promised that to his prayers he would add his own. The officer recovered. In gratitude he left the army and became a priest. Many years later he, him-

PIUS IX.

self, was elected Pope, and at once assumed the name of his benefactor, Pius; and he it was whose coming we expected every moment.

At length the sound of approaching steps was heard. The Papal Guards presented arms and Pius IX. appeared within the doorway. He was a handsome, well-preserved old man arrayed in white from head to foot. His manners were courteous and pleasing. Advancing toward us, with a charming smile, he said in French, "Ah, here are some good Americans who have come to see me." Then, after a few pleasant questions addressed to each of us about America and our stay in Rome, he passed on with his suite of cardinals, waving to us his blessing from a plump, white hand.

As for the present occupant of the Vatican, Leo XIII., St. Peter's chair has rarely held a broader-minded statesman. His views on social and political questions place him among the leading thinkers of the world. Moreover, he is a distinguished scholar. His tastes are highly intellectual; his letters and addresses are composed in elegant and polished Latin; and verses which he writes from time to time, in Latin or Italian, have earned for him the title of poet. Leo XIII. (as one who knew his private life

LEO XIII.

for seven years assured me) usually rises at six in the
morning.   At seven he says mass in his private chapel.
This is followed by a light breakfast.   Then he looks over his
letters and papers until the arrival of his Secretary of State
at nine.   The forenoon passes in conferences on State affairs
and in giving audiences.   At two o'clock he dines.   Only
a few are ever admitted to this repast, and they, according to
Papal etiquette, are not allowed to sit with the Holy Father,
but at a table just below him.   In the afternoon Leo descends
into the extensive gardens of the Vatican within the shaded
paths of which the Pontiff takes his only outdoor exercise.

THE GARDENS OF THE VATICAN.

THE VATICAN ENCLOSURE.

Here for an hour or two he walks or drives, noting with interest the cultivation of his trees and flowers. Then follow other audiences and religious consultations on important matters till evening. From that time on, until he retires, the Pope is always studying.

It is well known that since the creation of a united Italy, with Rome as its political capital, the Popes have never left the Vatican enclosure, remaining there in silent protest at their loss of temporal power. It is true the palace and its gardens are extensive; but, however large the cage and however beautiful its

THE LIBRARY OF THE VATICAN.

THE TRANSFIGURATION.

gilded bars, the eagle feels itself a captive still. Hence, there have doubtless been times in all these years when Leo XIII. has longed for greater liberty of movement, and in the sickening summer heat of Rome has pined for the pure breezes of his mountain home. The Italian Government, however, must feel relieved to have the Pope thus safely sheltered. What would not its responsibility and terror be, if Leo should walk out through the Eternal City in these appalling days of anarchism, bombs, and daggers?

The Vatican, quite apart from its religious associations, is of priceless value to the world as a colossal treasure-house of art, and offers to the visitor not only the amazing works of

A CORRIDOR OF STATUES.

Michelangelo in the Sistine Chapel, and the unrivaled frescos in the Stanze and Loggie of Raphael, but also a bewildering multitude of the statues of antiquity which have been rescued from Italian soil. I shall not soon forget my feeling of astonishment as I halted on the threshold of one corridor, in which nearly a thousand sculptured forms confronted me. When we consider that this is only one of many similar halls within the Vatican; that, besides all these, there are in the villas, palaces, and other galleries of art in Rome hundreds of other antique statues; and

THE APOLLO BELVEDERE.

that almost all the art museums in the world boast of some relics of the Eternal City, we may, perhaps, at first conclude that most of Rome's old treasures have escaped destruction.

But, notwithstanding all that has been brought to light, how little, after all, has been preserved to us! In the period of her glory it was said that the number of Rome's statues equaled that of her inhabitants, and even as late as the sixth century after Christ, when the magnificent old city had been repeatedly despoiled, a record of her then existing monuments mentions eighty gilded statues of gods, only one of which remains; sixty-six ivory statues of the deities, all of which are lost; three thousand seven hundred bronze figures, none of which can be accounted for; seventeen hundred palaces,

TREASURES OF THE PAST.

thirteen hundred fountains, nine hundred public baths, thirty-one theatres, and eight amphitheatres, all of which have fallen into complete or partial ruin! What has come down to us, therefore, is only the remnant of a mighty wreck, tossed on the shores of Time after the convulsions of a long-continued storm.

I left the Vatican and stood again beside the Tiber. The day was drawing to a close, and the entire city seemed pervaded

HADRIAN'S MAUSOLEUM AND ST. PETER'S.

with a violet haze which I could almost fancy the wraith of the imperial purple of the Palatine. Between me and the setting sun St. Peter's dome and Hadrian's mausoleum cut their majestic silhouettes against the sky, appropriate emblems of the two great kingdoms that have flourished here: those of the Cæsars and of Christ.

"You will soon take your leave of Rome," said my companion, " but be consoled, for Rome will not take leave of you."

I knew that he spoke truly, for to my lips the old Enchantress of the Seven Hills had held her magic cup, and I
had drunk too deeply ever to forget her. Her splendid churches,
classic statues, and imposing ruins will linger in my consciousness forevermore; and, henceforth, on the background of my
memory no grander figure will be visible than that of the former
Mistress of the World, wrapping about her wasted form the
tattered folds of an imperial mantle, yet proudly pointing her
enfeebled hand, upon which glitter side by side the signet of
the Cæsars and the jewel of the Papacy, — now toward her
glorious temples of Christianity, now toward the proofs of her
incomparable heritage of history, and her museums laden with
the spoils of Time.